OBEDIENT GERMANS?
A REBUTTAL

Studies in Early Modern German History

H. C. Eric Midelfort, Editor

OBEDIENT GERMANS?
A REBUTTAL

A New View of German History

(Deutsche Untertanen: Ein Widerspruch)

Peter Blickle

Translated by Thomas A. Brady Jr.

University Press of Virginia

Charlottesville and London

Publication of this translation was assisted by a grant from InterNationes.
Originally published in German as *Deutsche Untertanen: Ein Widerspruch*,
©1981 by Verlag C. H. Beck, München

The University Press of Virginia
Translation, Translator's Preface, and Translator's Introduction
© 1997 by the Rector and Visitors of the University of Virginia

Printed in the United States of America

First published 1997

∞ The paper used in this publication meets the minimum requirements
of the American National Standard for Information Sciences—Permanence
of Paper for Printed Library Materials, ANSI Z39.48-1984.

Library of Congress Cataloging-in-Publication Data
Blickle, Peter.
[Deutsche Untertanen. English]
Obedient Germans? : a rebuttal : a new view of German history / Peter Blickle ;
translated by Thomas A. Brady, Jr.
p.   cm. — (Studies in early modern German history)
Translation of: Deutsche Untertanen, 1981.
Includes bibliographical references and index.
ISBN 0-8139-1745-x (cloth : alk. paper)
ISBN 0-8139-1809-x (pbk : alk. paper)
I. Political participation—Germany—History. 2. Germany—History—1273–1517.
3. Germany—History—1517–1871. I. Title. II. Series.
JN3971.A91B5613   1997   97-26222
323'.042'0943—dc21   CIP

Contents

Illustrations

Plates

Figures

Translator's Preface

THIS TRANSLATION OWES its origin and completion to a long-held conviction, shared by the translator and the series' editor, that Peter Blickle's slim book on the Germans as obedient subjects merited translation into English. It offers a hypothesis about premodern Germany based on scholarship little known outside the German-speaking world in such a way as to make it accessible to the nonspecialist and the general reader of history. The most difficult aspect for the English-speaking reader arises from the heavy reliance of the German tradition of historical scholarship on institutions. Germany's premodern institutions reflected the country's political structure, which never assumed the relative uniformity one finds in English and French institutions of the same period. Blickle analyzes an institutional and linguistic multiplicity that was never refashioned by a centralizing monarchy.

To help the anglophone reader along these relatively unfamiliar ways, we have provided several aids. Explanations, especially of institutions, are provided in the translator's notes (identified by *"Tr. note"*), and a glossary of terms and suggestions for further reading are placed at the end of the text.

Some of the editorial policies in this translation require explanation. Parentheses appear as they did in the original, and square brackets are used for translator's interpolations. Personal and place-names are given in their original forms, except where standard English usage differs from German usage, for example, "Bavaria" for "Bayern" and "Saxony" for "Sachsen." Institutions lie at the heart of this work, and institutional terms posed the greatest problems of translation. The practice followed here is that an English rendering of the term is followed on first mention by the German original in parentheses. Where an explanation seems needed, it is provided in a translator's note. The bibliographical essay identifies only works in English and so is shorter.

Translator's Introduction:
A New View of German History

ONE DOES NOT HAVE to be particularly well read in modern European history to recognize the image of the Germans in modern times as a politically passive, even docile, people, who are more readily swayed than other Europeans by appeals to authoritarian values and methods. This image is often advanced to explain how a nation of philosophers and poets came to strive for world power and employ methods of a brutality rarely displayed by Europeans, at least in Europe. Often, an explanation for what the image teaches is found in the deeper German past: in the ancient Germanic experience in the primeval forests of northern Europe; in the Germans' failure to maintain a centralized state in the thirteenth century or to create a "new monarchy" in the sixteenth; in Martin Luther's implantation of authoritarian values in German minds; or in the political hegemony of militaristic Prussia.

These "explanations" began as justifications and became, in hostile hands, condemnations of modern Germany and the Germans, until the need to explain National Socialism forged them into the historical chain that William Shirer, among others, has made very widely known.[1] Implicating all of the German past, this orthodox image differs in one respect from the names hurled by one nationality at another in the deeper past, such as the "Cow Swiss" and "Pig Swabians" applied to one another by late-medieval Swiss stockmen and South German farmers, or the "toads" and "goddamns" used by British and French soldiers during the revolutionary wars. It differs in that this long-standard account of German history partakes of the modern racialist faith, the touching belief in the immutability of collective mentalities through history.

Arguments of this kind are not peculiar to German history. Many other current debates displace themselves into the deep and deeper past, either to show how marvelously the present has advanced over a horrifying past or to show that present horrors are the consequence of a false turn in history. The search for German origins nevertheless gains an especially urgent quality from the need to explain National Socialism, and it refashions all of the older myths to its service, no matter how often or how well the historians have debunked them. This urgency lends a special relevance to Peter Blickle's *Obedient Germans? A Rebuttal*, which aims to refute this view of German history as a headlong march of an unrelentingly authoritarian people toward National Socialism.

Blickle's target is not the actual search for the origins of National Socialism but the related, older view of German history as centered on the formation of a strong state. This view was until fairly recently the canonical one in the German historical establishment, descended as it was from Leopold von Ranke (1795–1886) and Heinrich von Treitschke (1834–1896). They and their disciples saw the High Middle Ages as the springtime and the nineteenth century as the summer of German state-building. They saw these two eras as divided, in a curious perversion of the seasonal cycle, by the long autumn of five centuries between 1250 and 1750, roughly the time span treated by *Obedient Germans? A Rebuttal*. During these centuries, while other European nations were building strong states and gaining overseas empires, the orthodoxy ran, the Germans languished in political fragmentation—called "particularism"—that was perpetuated by the Roman papacy's opposition to the Protestant Reformation. The resulting weakness opened Germany to the foreign military intervention that transformed a German civil war into the catastrophe of the Thirty Years' War.[2] Not until the mid–eighteenth century did the rise of a new military power, Prussia, begin to reverse this long decline and to lead the Germans toward the new Germany established in 1871.[3]

Not only did this established narrative measure the progress toward strong statehood against the western European national histories, but its intense concentration on the unitary nation-state as the goal of German history encouraged Germans to regard the five hundred years between 1250 and 1750 as a time of lost opportunities and misdirections—in short, a historical injustice to be made good.

There were always dissenters from this way of seeing things, of course, but the only serious pre–1914 challenger, Karl Lamprecht (1856–1915), proved an easy target for his critics because of his cavalier research methods.[4] After 1918 it was a very different story: the Great War proved the fragility, even mortality, of modern states, and during the 1920s the prestige of the sovereign, unitary, national state was eroding in several European countries.[5] In the German-speaking world the major blow came at the hands of an Austrian medievalist, Otto Brunner, whose *"Land" and Lordship*, published in 1939, achieved "a radical reevaluation of medieval constitutional forms and liberated the language of medieval constitutional history from the juristic conceptual schemes of the nineteenth and twentieth centuries."[6] Brunner attacked the practice of writing medieval constitutional history solely based on its relevance to the evolution of the modern (European) state and its defining characteristics of full external and internal sovereignty, explicitly defined boundaries, and a clear distinction between the realms of public and private law that defined the respective fields of action of the state and the citizen.

Against the established view of a long development toward a German national state, Brunner posed the demand that "studies concerned with medieval politics must somehow account for the fact that political action, even warfare, existed not only between medieval 'states' but also within them."[7] The legal institution of the feud, he argued, demonstrates that medieval German bodies were entirely different in character from modern sovereign states. Their law, which arose from the political community of the territory or "land," did not exclude violence on the part of the members and was not grounded in any specific law—positive, natural, or divine—but in a undefined but legitimating sense of "right" (*Recht*).

Drawing on records from the regions of Austro-Bavarian speech and influenced, almost certainly, by his antidemocratic bias, Brunner argued that armed landholders, or knights, formed the medieval political community,

Thomas A. Brady Jr.

and that later incorporations of monasteries, towns, and even peasants into it by means of parliamentary estates were to be regarded as a kind of degeneration. Yet his view of the householder's exclusive authority over the household as the ultimate legal sources of all lordship allowed the inference that the noble land-community was but one way of constituting medieval government, which did not in principle have to rest on the nobles' lordship over peasants. Indeed, Brunner's recognition of the late medieval Swiss powers as genuine "lands" confirmed the possibility that burghers and even peasants could constitute genuine governments.[8]

Brunner's attack on the view that development toward the unitary national state was the core of German history forms one part of the background to Peter Blickle's argument in *Obedient Germans? A Rebuttal*. A second part, which also took shape during the interwar era, arose from historical study of German rural life. The older legal historians, notably Georg Ludwig von Maurer (1790–1872) and Otto von Gierke (1841–1921), had recognized that politically capable communal associations had formed in the countryside during the Middle Ages. It was twentieth-century legal historian Karl Siegfried Bader who laid bare in three volumes the forms and procedures of late medieval village self-government.[9] He thus demonstrated that the historical interventions of peasants, like those of burghers, were not inexplicable "natural events" (Ranke's term)[10] but manifestations of a long tradition of political experience and definite political goals.

These ideas, plus more than a Marxist whiff of history as the history of class conflict, flow together to form the basis in Blickle's *Obedient Germans? A Rebuttal* of a new view of German history. It is the story of struggle between two socially differentiated forces. The first is noble authoritarianism, which produced the absolutist states of the eighteenth century and, by implication, continued to influence German political development in more recent times. The second force is popular communalism, which provided the historic resistance to absolutism and, by implication, formed the historical background to modern German democracy. The struggle between the two began in the century or more after 1250, when the long economic

Translator's Introduction

depression first brought rights of self-government into the hands of burghers and farmers, thereby creating the social basis of an opposition to noble domination. The deep devolution of governance during the later Middle Ages—as "particularism" long scorned by nationally minded historians—thus created in Blickle's view the popular challenge to authoritarian rule in Germany. Its agents were the common people—the burghers and the farmers—and their characteristic mode of political behavior was not obedience but assertion of their rights and resistance to all who threatened those rights.

Peter Blickle's small, potent book challenges directly one of the most cherished of modern dogmas about the political behavior of the Germans: that they are peculiarly susceptible, because of their historical experience, to passivity toward authoritarian regimes. This dogma was created by nationalist historians, jurists, and propagandists to justify the "revolution from above" that created Bismarck's new Germany in 1871; it was embellished and exploited by authoritarian nationalists from that time until 1945; and it has been adopted and adapted by Germany's critics and enemies since at least 1914 and perhaps before. Without apologizing for the violent events and movements of modern German history, Blickle aims to show that they represent the perversion of German political tradition, not its outcome, that the Germans learned early and well how to govern themselves, and that for most of their history they were anything but obedient Germans.

Notes

1. See Uwe Siemon-Netto, *The Fabricated Luther: The Rise and Fall of the Shirer Myth* (St. Louis, 1995), who added William Shirer to his gallery of targets in the English edition. Mainly a shortsighted apology for Luther, the book ignores the larger German context of the national myth.

2. There is no better formulation of the historical foundations of this vision than the original one by Leopold von Ranke, *History of the Reformation in Germany*, translated by Sarah Austin (London, 1905), esp. 20, 29–39, 115–22, 316–33. On Ranke, see Leonard Krieger, *Ranke: The Meaning of History* (Chicago, 1977), by far the best treatment of Ranke in English.

3. This was the basic story told by the tradition of nationalist historical writing that has been called "the German conception of History." See Georg G. Iggers, *The German Conception of History: The National Tradition of Historical Thought from Herder to the Present*, 2d ed. (Middletown CT, 1988).

4. Thus the estimate of Roger Chickering, *Karl Lamprecht: A German Academic Life (1856–1915)* (Atlantic Highlands NJ, 1993), esp. 108–11.

5. It has been recognized that Brunner's work bears a kinship to the approach to history voiced and practiced by the founders of the *Annales* in France. This applies both to Marc Bloch, who disrupted the antiseptic legalism of the old, purely institutional concept of feudalism, and to Lucien Febvre, who taught that for historians the unforgivable sin is anachronism. See Hartmut Lehmann and James Van Horn Melton, eds., *Paths of Continuity: Central European Historiography from the 1930s to the 1950s* (Cambridge MA, 1994), and especially Melton's valuable study of Brunner.

6. Robert Jütte, "Zwischen Ständestaat und Austrofaschismus. Der Beitrag Otto Brunners zur Geschichtsschreibung," *Jahrbuch des Instituts für Deutsche Geschichte* 13 (1984): 237–62. The book in question is Otto Brunner, *"Land" and Lordship: Structures of Governance in Medieval Austria*, translated by Howard Kaminsky and James Van Horn Melton (Philadelphia, 1992). See my evaluation of the translation in "Whose Land? Whose Lordship? The New Translation of Otto Brunner: A Review Article," *Central European History* 29 (1996): 227–34.

7. Brunner, *"Land" and Lordship*, 3–4.

8. Brunner's identification of the household, not the citizen, as the political bedrock of medieval "lands" also poses another possibility, which he ignored, of exploring the gender relations that lay at the root of all lordship. This path untaken by Brunner has been pioneered with great effect by David W. Sabean, *Property, Production, and Family in Neckarhausen* (Cambridge MA, 1991).

9. Karl Siegfried Bader, *Studien zur Rechtsgeschichte des mittelalterlichen Dorfes*, 3 vols. (Vienna, 1957–73).

10. Leopold von Ranke, *Deutsche Geschichte im Zeitalter der Reformation*, edited by Willy Andreas, 2 vols. (Wiesbaden, n.d.), 1:317, called the German Peasants' War a "*Naturereignis*," which translator Sarah Austin rendered in the English edition as "elemental strife" (Ranke, *History of the Reformation in Germany*, 351).

Viewed politically, the German was and is the very embodiment of the "subject" in the word's most poignant sense.

Max Weber

Power is inherently evil.

Jakob Burckhardt

Foreword

THE FOLLOWING REFLECTIONS STEM from a lecture I gave in the summer semester of 1980 as a farewell to my Saarbrücken students. They wanted me to summarize the research I conducted during my Saarbrücken years and to place it in the larger context of German history. The undertaking was problematical, because it required me to cast my work in terms of brief theses and abbreviated models. Yet it was important to my role as a teacher to convey in this form my understanding of historical scholarship, which has the task of reconstructing the past on historical principles connected to the present, so that history does not remain an antiquarian curiosity.

Once I had decided to develop and publish my lecture—the subject had never been treated in a monograph—it appeared to be important enough for a wider audience. I was able to draw upon the discussion in recent years of the complex of concepts subject–peasant–common man. I developed it in a polemical, partly apologetical way, hoping thereby to defend uncommon views that run against the conventional interpretations of German social and constitutional history. Since I wanted also to bring this problem to the attention of scholarly discussion, it seemed legitimate to try to bring the individual strands together into a coherent interpretation and to test its utility for the explanation of German history.

This task and its preliminary stages have determined this volume's form and contents. It is an extended essay not only because of its length but because of my aim to present clearly in a comprehensible way some arguments which seem important. I have thus deliberately favored generalization over qualification. The argument's stronger focus on rural than on urban society arises from the subject itself, because in a society that was still over-whelmingly agrarian, the majority of the subjects consisted of peasants. Further, this focus reflects my own scholarly work, which I hope has been adequate to convey the basic problems of the subject. I present here further reflections on older research rather than elements of new research. The cumulative character of historical knowledge makes it legitimate to formulate and present discussible theses at any time, especially when, as I believe to be the case here, the topic has been at best neglected and at worst rejected from historical consciousness altogether.

Saarbrücken, October 1980

Introduction

The Concepts of "Subjects" and "Rulers"

A "SUBJECT," as defined by a recently published dictionary, is "a dependent of a preconstitutional, usually absolutist, state."[1] Ever since the French Revolution the term "subject" has been generally replaced by that of the "citizen" in the sense of the French *citoyen*, so as to emphasize democratic popular sovereignty. "Subject" is defined in German as belonging to the preconstitutional, premodern state. In Germany the concept developed under the princely state, that is, under the territorial state as it developed since the late Middle Ages within the Holy Roman Empire of the German Nation. Although the definition of the term is neutral, today "subject" bears a pejorative connotation because it suggests servility and the avoidance of political responsibility.

In Germany the best-known literary example of this meaning is the title of Heinrich Mann's (1871–1950) novel, *The Subject (Der Untertan)*. Politically critical German writers complain of the subject mentality as a typical defect of the Germans. "Mommy! Mommy!" cries the young boy, "Georgie keeps hitting me! He says I should sit in the trash can and sing 'The Watch on the Rhine'! We're playing soldier. I don't want to sit in the trash can, Mommy!" The mother replies, "Why do you do what he says, you dummy, you yellow-belly (*oller Dösknochen, oller Schlappschwanz*)!' Suddenly enlightened, the young boy responds, "Because he's my boss."[2] These lines from a story by Kurt Tucholsky (1890–1935) convey an idea often met with in German literature, and such passages comprise but one expression of a general displeasure with what might be captured within the polemical dyad, the "subject mentality" and the "authoritarian state." In this light, not coincidentally, President Gustav Heinemann (1899–1976) of the German Federal Republic felt compelled to warn his fellow Germans: "I believe that it speaks poorly for a democratic society when even today rebellious peasants are regarded as nothing more than mutinous mobs, who should be tamed and caged by the state."[3] Such a comment presumes that the history of the broad masses in Germany—Heinemann was looking back to the Peasants' War of 1525—was characterized by absolute passivity and silent obedience, the classic virtues of a subject.

In words that also appear as this book's epigraph, sociologist Max Weber (1864–1920) anticipated Mann, Tucholsky, and Heinemann with the remark that "the German" is "the very embodiment of the 'subject.'" Weber grounded his view in history, noting that the subject was a part, if not necessarily a product, of the premodern, patrimonial state, and because this type of state endured longer in Germany than in the rest of Europe, and "from a political viewpoint the German has indeed been the typical subject (*Untertan*) in the most poignant sense of the word."[4] The concept of the "subject" was connected from the outset, in Weber's view, with political "immaturity" and "dependence," because the premodern, patrimonial state was an authoritarian form of rule that rested on the army and the bureaucracy alone. The historical accuracy of Weber's analysis can be demonstrated from eighteenth-century Germany, which was still a premodern society, organized by legally defined estates.[5] The most comprehensive eighteenth-century German lexicon, which dedicates a respectable forty columns to the idea of "subject," introduces the term in lapidary fashion: "Subjects are all who are subordinated to a ruler and are bound to obey his laws and commands."[6] To be sure, subjects possess "traditional rights and liberties," which should not be violated "except in cases of urgent necessity," but "if the common good requires their restriction or abolition, the territorial ruler may restrict or abolish them in good conscience." If his conscience bothers him—the author allows this possibility—the subjects may "humbly describe their rights with appropriate reasons and may seek to deter their ruler's intended action by begging and pleading. If this does not work, however, and the ruler persists, they must obey, for they have no right to resist." Such was the characteristic view of the subject in the age of absolutism. The subject had a duty to obey but no right to resist, and the ruler's conscience was the only check on the ruler's power—a check, history shows, of doubtful efficacy.

This interpretation nonetheless met with strong opposition from the eighteenth century onward, as it must have done, whenever and wherever there arose a desire for mature citizenship and democracy. "Citizen" and "subject" thus are contradictory terms. "I must protest, Sir," says the marquis in Friedrich von Schiller's *Don Carlos*, "that I, a citizen of this world, am not prepared to clothe my ideas in your subject's words."

This negative concept of the subject has predominated from the late eighteenth century to the present. Because the historical discipline emerged during the same age, it is hardly surprising that the subject has not been a proper theme for historical writing, because servility and the avoidance of responsibility were hardly categories which could shape and structure the historical process.

This book deals with the German subject in the narrow and precise sense of the term—the subject of the preconstitutional state, those persons whom the emperors and princes could call "subjects" without fear of contradiction and who even called themselves "subjects." The terminology needs to be examined more precisely than it has been in the past.

The term "subject" can be first documented in the fourteenth century. At that time the concept had two meanings, one broad and one narrow. The broad meaning virtually reproduced the word's original suggestion that the political or social world contained an "above" and a "below." "Subject" in this sense was a functional, constitutional concept, as revealed in this eighteenth–century statement: "Subjection and rule stood in contrast to each other in a most precise relationship, so that there could be no subject without a ruler and, conversely, no ruler without subjects." In the complex constitutional architecture of the Holy Roman Empire, there were different levels of subjects because there were different levels of rulers or governance (*Herrschaft*). An elector was the emperor's subject, a peasant was his master's subject. The recess of the Imperial Diet of 1471 notes the emperor's connections to "prelates, counts, barons, knights, squires, mayors, councillors, cities, communes, and other aforementioned subjects."[7]

The second, narrower meaning of "subject" corresponds more closely to the term's generally accepted modern meaning. In a colloquial and oversimplified way, we might refer to subjects today as "the commoners" or the "ordinary people." Ever since the later Middle Ages, the word "subject" has been increasingly used in this narrow sense to designate the peasants of the countryside and the burghers of the towns. The nobles and upper clergy consistently refused to be included in the term. This distinction reflects the main line of development of governance in the Holy Roman Empire, which can be summed up as follows.

In the empire, states developed in the territories of those rulers—electors, dukes, counts, bishops, prelates, and free cities—who, because they stood directly under the emperor and were therefore with some exceptions called to attend the imperial parliament or diet, were called "imperial estates" (*Reichsstände*). Gradually, the complex forms of rule known during the High Middle Ages became simpler and more uniform in the princely "territorial state," which evolved into the archetypal form of "early modern state" in the empire. Burghers and peasants became the subjects of this early modern state ruled by a prince (the same is roughly true for the territories of the free cities). This term, "subject," nevertheless does not adequately and fully describe the political status of the late medieval and early modern rural and urban populations. Contemporaries also called such folk "the common man."

The terms "subject" and "the common man" were nearly synonymous. The recess of the Imperial Diet of Speyer in 1526 remarked that "although the common man and subject forgot their obligations in the recent upheaval and acted against their rulers, yet, in order that they may experience their ruler's grace and mercy more freely and fully than their irrational deeds would warrant, every ruler shall be empowered to restore to their former honorable status those subjects who surrender without conditions and who have been punished for their deeds. They are further empowered to restore such subjects to posts in the councils and courts and to allow them to testify in court and to hold offices."[8] "Subject" and "common man" maintained this equivalency for centuries, as can be seen in a pair of passages dated more than four centuries apart: in the mid–fifteenth century the abbot of the Swabian abbey of Rot designated his serfs and tenants "subjects"; in 1872 Otto von Bismarck addressed the Roman Catholics in the Prussian House of Delegates, hoping "to find a buttress for the government in a loyally Catholic party, the members of which are willing to render unto Caesar what is Caesar's and seek to maintain respect for the government, even when they believe it to have erred, in all social classes, that is, in those of the politically less well-informed common man, namely, the masses."[9]

The term "subject" was used more often than "the common man," and this preference, which is also visible in the scholarship, undoubtedly reflects the strengthening of the state and a growing emphasis on its authoritarian character. Despite the limitations of space here, it is nonetheless profitable to clarify the terms by means of etymological and conceptual analysis.

The earliest evidence for the term "common man" comes from an Erfurt compilation of customary law (*Weistum*) of 1289 under the heading of "Head Tax" (*Schlagschatz*): "No one shall be exempt from the head tax, neither priest nor layman, neither noble nor commoner."[10] Clergy and laity, nobles and the common man, are here conceived as pairs of contraries, and "commoner" must refer to both burghers and peasants. Here and elsewhere—as in the Golden Bull of 1356 or in Albert II's public peace of 1438—"the common man" served as a collective term for the nonnoble members of the population.[11]

Indeed, in terms of status and social position the concept of the common man was bounded only at its upper edge by the status of nobility. Numerous sixteenth-century texts show clearly that burghers and peasants were considered, respectively, the urban and the rural elements of the common man.[12] One text speaks, for example, of "the common man in the cities and in the countryside," while another complains that "the common man can bring the clergyman and the nobleman to law only with great difficulty and at heavy cost." The imperial free cities' envoys to the Imperial Diet voiced the fear that "rebellion and hatred might arise between the rulers and the common man in the cities." Later centuries, however, supply evidence for the cities' efforts to avoid using the concept of the common man to designate their own inhabitants because the term became increasingly restricted to the rural populations. Thus, already at the beginning of the seventeenth century, the district assembly (*Banntaiding*) of the Lower Austrian district of Stickelberg distinguished sharply between burghers and nonburghers: "When the assembly is called and a burgher fails to appear, he shall pay 6 Crowns, whereas a common man shall pay 3 Crowns."[13] Later, a text of 1730 from the county of Nassau-Saarbrücken declared that "the common man subsists mostly from raising livestock."[14] At the same time "the common man" was being restricted to the peasantry, the term "subject" also contracted to designate the same people. This change was noted at the time by Württemberg jurist Johann Jacob Moser (1701–1785), who wrote that "some wish to narrow the meaning of this term to the peasants as the lowest stratum of subjects." He nonetheless rejected this contraction, commenting, "But I know of no land in which the official language recognizes this usage, [since] those inhabitants of the free cities, who are not burghers, are also subjects."[15]

The evidence of usage supplied by these texts allows us to define our topic more precisely in three respects. First, the widespread identification of the subject with the common man permits us to exclude from our analysis the broader sense of the concept of subject as referring to any dependent of any ruler. Second, the gradual restriction of both terms to mean the rural people may justify concentrating our analysis more on the village than on the town. And third, the primary contrast between the subject or the common man and the ruler suggests that we should focus our political analysis on the relations between subjects and rulers.

Where can we locate the government (*Obrigkeit*) of premodern Germany? Research on territorial and constitutional history has yielded the conclusion that from the later Middle Ages onward, statelike government developed in the empire's territories.[16] Emperor and empire lost their statelike functions to the territorial princes and the territories, or at least they were unable to construct a comparable and rival concentration of powers. This means that the theme of the subject must be examined and analyzed primarily on the territorial, not on the imperial, level. This was well known to the eighteenth-century jurists. In his introduction to his *On the Rights and Obligations of German Subjects* (*Von der Teutschen Unterthanen Rechten und Pflichten*), Johann Jacob Moser wrote that "I understand as 'German subjects' those inhabitants and members of the German Empire who do not stand immediately under the emperor and the Roman Empire, but under an imperial estate."[17] Nevertheless the empire, as we shall see, cannot be left entirely out of account, nor can the seigneuries and lordships within the territories. Indeed, the latter, depending on their institutional development, could sometime become full-fledged rulers. The Junkers of seventeenth- and eighteenth-century Mecklenburg, for example, did so with respect to their servile peasantry.

The Holy Roman Empire formed a political hierarchy: above the local nobles and other lords stood territorial rulers, and above the latter stood the empire. In this triad of local nobleman—territorial ruler—emperor, the territorial government was normally both the strongest component and the one capable of greatest growth. For this reason our analysis of the topic of the subject has to focus on the primarily political relationship between the subject and the territorial state. More precisely, it must concentrate on what rights the subjects possessed in the kind of state that is called "territorial." In their social status and condition, 85 to 90 percent of the empire's inhabitants were peasants, or, more precisely, rural inhabitants. Another 10 to 12 percent consisted of burghers or, more precisely, townsmen. What significance did such folk have for the state or in the state? They were payers of taxes and other dues, and they were a labor force, but were they not more? Did they not have a political history in which they appear as actors, or were they merely the objects of someone else's political history?

In the Holy Roman Empire the bipolar relationship between subject and the territorial state lasted from the fourteenth century to the empire's collapse in 1806. This is the period of what in social and constitutional terms is called "the state based on social orders (or estates)."[18] In such a state, orders or estates, such as the nobility, the clergy, and the burghers, claimed certain political rights and, when legally constituted as estates, exercised their rights and represented their claims in territorial parliaments. In social terms, in a late medieval state based on orders, people were relegated to a specific order. "God created three ways of life," declared one text, those of "peasants, knights, and priests." Everyone belonged to the peasant order, the noble order, or the priestly order, which undertook the three functional tasks—

Plate 1. Those who pray, those who fight, those who work. The estates (clergy, nobles, peasants) as a divinely willed social order. From Johann Lichtenberger, *Prognosticatio* (Mainz, Jakob Meydenbach, 1492), fol. 6.

work, defense, and prayer—that medieval society allotted to specific social groups, reckoning people as members of either the producing, the defensive, or the sacerdotal orders (plate 1). From the original formulation of this simple idea in the eleventh century, an increasingly complex division of labor gave rise to a division of the producing order into two estates, peasants and burghers. The original unity of the two, however, was preserved in the concepts of subjects and the common man, and it was rooted in their common activity, their labor, which distinguished them from the two higher, nonproducing estates, the nobles and the clergy.

The articulation of German society into estates or orders was not complete until around 1300. In the documents of this time the terms "warriors" (*milites*) and "farmers" (*rustici*) replace the older social categories of "free" and "unfree." At about the same time, the city with its burghers emerged as an order separate from the previously recognized orders of nobles (with the clergy) and peasants. At this time, too, the peasant first appeared in the documents as a social type. A characteristic figure of the society based on orders, he was defined as a producer of vegetable and animal foodstuffs from a self-sufficient economic unit, the family farm, a unit of both production and consumption managed by the peasant himself. The surplus he produced, beyond his investment and operating costs, supported the ruling orders of nobility and clergy. Much later, during the nineteenth century, this social order and its specific meaning of "peasant" were destroyed through the emancipation of the peasants, that is, the abolition of their legal and financial subordination to intermediate authorities, such as nobles and abbeys. In the nineteenth century the privileged orders of nobles and clergy also lost their functions in public law, while their rights in private law were either commuted to cash payments or compensated through state-financed redemptions of their rights in the land. The free farmer on his freehold then merged with the urban burgher into the modern citizen, while the early modern state was simultaneously transformed from a state based on orders into a modern, constitutional state. These events provide us with a chronological framework, roughly the time between 1300 and 1800, for our study of obedient and disobedient subjects in Germany.

Introduction

Over the course of this half-millennium unfolded a fascinating story of the struggles between rulers and subjects over the material basis, functional division, and ethical justification for the expansion of the state. The story proceeded on two different but related political levels, one of "positive integration" on the local level of the commune (chapter 1) and on the territorial level of the parliamentary assembly *Landschaft* (chapter 2), and the other as "negative integration" in the form of revolts (chapter 3). These three elements—communal formation, political representation, and popular revolts—make up the Germans' "history" as obedient subjects, which I demonstrate to be a contradiction in terms.

Chapter 1

The Commune
as a Political Association

At the turn from the High to the later Middle Ages around 1300, Central Europe underwent a decisive political and social change that produced what may be called "the formation of communes." Associative bodies developed that both claimed by right and undertook to perform tasks of a political nature. Nothing so sweeping had happened during the preceding era, the High Middle Ages, when the dominant social and political order had been organized into a vertical hierarchy. Under such conditions, the tiniest form of horizontally configured association—such as the association of manorial dependents (*Fronhofsgenossenschaft*)—understood itself in terms defined solely by its relationship to the lord's manor. The associations of that earlier era, therefore, were formed on the principle of lordship alone, whereas those of the later Middle Ages were based on the associative principle of the neighborhood. These neighborhood associations could take different forms, such as valley communes, mountain communes, rural districts, and urban communes. In the history of one such form, the village commune, we can trace clearly the late medieval social transformation of "the ruled" or "the subjects."

The Emergence of the Village and the Commune

Around 1300 the village and the commune emerged as mutually dependent institutions.[1] Historians and archaeologists now reject the nineteenth-century view that the village can be traced back into the Germanic, that is, premedieval, era, since we are now certain that the village owes its historic shape, if not its physical origin, to the era around 1300. The emergence of the village around this time reflects important changes in the patterns of settlement, in economic organization and techniques, in social order, and in the structure of governance.

The Commune as a Political Association

Changes in Settlement

Writing of the Swiss-Alemannic settlement region,[2] Rogier Sablonier has asserted that "it was only during the High Middle Ages that the settlement patterns became stable, both in the regions characterized by individual farms and dispersed settlements and in those where the village predominated. Before this era, we find a more or less dense, fluctuating pattern of settlement in hamlets or groups of farmsteads."[3] Regional differences aside, this observation applies to all of Germany. Studies on settlement in western and northern Germany have shown that the nucleated village (*Haufendorf*), once held to be of early Germanic origin, did not appear before the High Middle Ages, that is, in the tenth through the twelfth centuries. Archaeologists have also established that the small settlement was dominant in the empire's southern regions even before then.

The reasons for this intensification and crystallization of settlements have not been satisfactorily established. Economic and political forces, to be considered below, played their parts in this fundamental change, but so did changes in mentality, which expressed themselves in significant changes in methods of house construction. The replacement of flimsy temporary structures (*Gruben- und Pfostenhäuser*) by sturdy, permanent houses on stone foundations (*Ständerhäuser*) seems to correspond to a coagulation of earlier forms of settlement into the nucleated village and thus to an increasingly sedentary rural population.

Similar changes can be documented in the church. The founding of many churches and chapels about this time indicates an intensification of formerly loose networks of social communication and the appearance of new religious and social needs. At least in the empire's southwestern regions, the ecclesiastical topography attained by 1300 a state that has never since undergone marked change. The social association of sedentary peasants in the village thereby became a religious association as well, the consequences of which can only be suggested here. In the main, it meant a definitive Christianization of the countryside, a process by which for the first time peasants came into contact with the larger cultural institutions of the age. The reduction of this isolation had far-reaching consequences, including, as we shall see, the capacity for criticizing the existing social and political order.

The Commune as a Political Association

Changes in Agriculture

The formation of the village also reveals a fundamental change in the methods and organization of agriculture. Documents around 1300 refer more frequently to village boundaries, suggesting that the zones claimed by villages now abutted one another, a sign of growing population and decreasing reserves of land. The necessarily more intensive exploitation of scarcer resources probably lay behind the organization of the village's lands into three closely related "concentric, legally defined circles," which together defined the village. These were the nuclear village proper (*Siedlung*), the croplands (*bebaute Flur*), and the pastures and woodlands that made up the commons (*Allmende*). This triple differentiation by function is of great interest, because it explains why the village could develop functions that may be called "governmental" (*staatlich*).

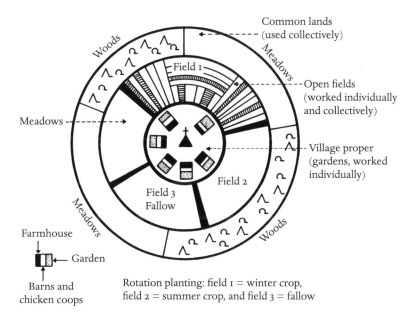

Fig. 1. Model of a village. The shaded portions in Field 1 show which fields Farmhouse A might own.

The three concentric circles of the village lands can be described as follows. The first circle (A) formed the farmsteads in the narrower sense, each consisting of a house, courtyard, and garden. This was the center of the farmer's individual enterprise to a degree that, following Karl Siegfried Bader, we may almost speak of "private property."

The second circle (B) comprised the cropland, which was exploited in part individually and in part collectively by the village. Individual exploitation took place basically during the months between planting and harvest, while after the harvest the village householders used the land collectively as pasturage.

The third circle (C), the commons, consisted of woodlands and pasture, which were subject only to collective exploitation. The woods, far from a monoculture of the modern kind, consisted of a mixed forest that supplied the farmers' hogs with acorns and beechnuts and the farmsteads with building timber, firewood, and fencing material. The farmers used the pastures collectively for their livestock.

This relatively complex combination of individual and collective exploitation developed historically from the convergence of three processes: the shift from cattle-raising to cultivation of grain (*Vergetreidung*), the shift to the three-field system (*Verzelgung*), and the dissolution of the manorial system (*Villikation*).

The chief cause of the shift from cattle to grain was doubtless the growth of population during the High Middle Ages, because the caloric yield per acre of cropland is many times higher than that of pasture. In order to obtain maximum use of the land, the nucleation of villages was accompanied by a more intensive system of crop rotation, often in the form of the three-field system (*Dreizelgenwirtschaft*) based on the annual rotation of winter crops, summer crops, and fallow to regenerate the soil. This could not be introduced by individual farmers, because in common-field farming the preparation, sowing, and harvesting of the fields had to be accomplished by collective effort. The consequent need for agreement and cooperation brought all farmers under a cultivation schedule (*Flurzwang*). The shifts toward grain and toward coordinated cultivation, themselves consequences of rising demand for foodstuffs, led to a sharper distinction between plowland

and pasture. Where possible, crops replaced pasture, which survived only to supply farmers with fodder and manure.

Possibly the most important prerequisite to the formation of the village was the dissolution of the old manorial order.[4] That order had rested on the reservation of an extensive parcel, called the demesne (*Salland*), which was directly cultivated for the lord by means of labor services (*Dienste, Fronen*) owed by the farmers. The dissolution of the manorial system meant parceling out and leasing the domain and thus suppressing labor dues. This process introduced a decisive social change on the land.

Changes in Social Organization

The village in the sense defined above developed at the same time that the agricultural organization was shifting from direct to indirect exploitation, roughly the era of transition from the High to the later Middle Ages. The shift forced corresponding changes in the organization of the manor. In the old manorial order, the demesne was cultivated by means of the labor services performed by servile farmers under the leadership of the lord or his bailiff (*villicus*), and the lord or seigneur could in principle command his unfree dependents' labor power at will. In the new system of indirect exploitation, by contrast, the tenants paid (largely fixed) rents to the lord in cash and kind. This meant that the lord's demesne was now exploited indirectly, parceled out and leased in units large enough to sustain a household-based agriculture. In principle, therefore, labor services disappeared, so that the hitherto-unfree farmer now commanded his own labor. This turned the previously servile farmer into a peasant in the classic sense of the term.

We can give this model of transition from direct to indirect exploitation greater complexity and greater proximity to reality by recognizing that peasant farms had also existed under the manorial system. These were leaseholds for a stipulated number of years, or at most for life, and when the lease expired or the tenant died, the farm and the tenant's personal property reverted to the lord. This practice gave the lord something like an unlimited claim to the fruits of the unfree tenant's labor. According to the manorial system's logic, labor power and the fruits of labor were two sides of the same coin, behind which stood the German lord's right to claim any surplus beyond the tenant's costs.

Following the transition to indirect exploitation in the German-speaking lands, farms formerly rented on less advantageous terms were generally let on hereditary leases, a tendency that also spread to the holdings created by carving up the lords' demesnes. This shift toward heritable leases meant that farms now passed from father to son and could remain for generations in the same family, and that, once fixed, rents could rarely be raised significantly. Thus, except for the rents he owed, the peasant came to command the fruits of his own labor.

Gaining a free command over one's own labor and its fruits marked a great turning point in the history of the organization of labor. Indeed, the only comparable change in European history has been the subsequent transition from the society based on orders, with its corporately organized, self-regulated labor of peasants and artisans, to the industrial age's system of wage labor. Socially, the late medieval change meant the passage from unfreedom to freedom, from rule by others to self-rule, and it naturally brought far-reaching political changes, as well.

Changes in Government

These changes in settlement, notably the multiplication of nuclei, created a great many new needs for regulation. In agriculture, as we have seen, the lord's withdrawal from the direct management of farming led to a village economy based on a combination of individual and collective enterprise. We can interpret the social changes produced by this individualization of labor as the coming of what may be described as a kind of freedom.

Because the manor's decay left few or no established political and administrative institutions, many social and economic tasks were shifted to the newly created unit of the village. The intensification of social relations and the growing complexity of the economy required new norms for living in close company and for institutions to punish violations of such norms within the village. The new norms arose from what in modern language is called the legislative power (*Gebots- und Verbotsgewalt*) of the village commune

(*Dorfgemeinde*); from the need to enforce the village's ordinances arose administrative organs in the form of village offices; and from the need to clarify the norms arose the village court (*Dorfgericht*).

The manor's role as the central form of rural social organization in earlier times enables us to understand the village as a continuation, branch, or transformation of the manor, from which it inherited its functions. We can easily trace the lines of continuity from the manorial constitution to the village constitution: manorial law "found" by the manorial association (*familia*) corresponded to the later law framed by the village association;[5] and the old manorial court with or without judges (*Schöffen*) corresponded to the later village court with judges (*Schöffengericht*).

Under the manorial system, of course, the lord or seigneur had enjoyed a dominant position because of his exclusive authority to make ordinances and to preside over the manorial court. This background explains the twofold roots, one communal-associative and the other seigneurial, of the functions that came to be exercised in the village by villagers.[6] It also explains how the various configurations of dividing authority between the village's commune and its lord led in practice to many different ways of separating functions within the village.

Despite this diversity, it is nonetheless possible to present a schematic diagram of a typical village's institutional structure (fig. 2). The central organ of self-government in the village was the communal assembly (*Gemeindeversammlung*), in which the full members of the commune gathered at least once a year, sometimes more frequently. Its task was to audit the commune's finances (*Rechnungsabhör*), to fix the rotation of croplands among two, three, or more fields, to proclaim and record village law (*Weistum*), and to elect the commune's officers.

The most important officers elected by the communal assembly were "the Four" (sometimes "the Three," "the Five," "the Twelve," "the Sworn Ones," or "the Council"), whose name derives from their original number of four and reveals the office's collegial character. They represented for certain purposes the whole community and supervised all its tasks: verification of the boundaries of land parcels and the district itself; provision for the fire watch; supervision of weights and measures; oversight of village crafts; and

The Commune as a Political Association

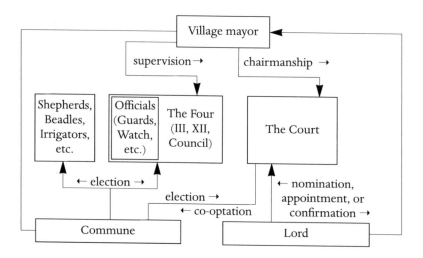

Fig. 2. The self-government of a village commune.

general supervision of the mill, the tavern, the smithy, and the bathhouse. Though the bundle of tasks varied from commune to commune and from village to village, this group of magistrates functioned in most cases as the commune's supervisory organ, and it also acquired judicial functions. Depending on the commune's size, some of these tasks could be delegated to special officers: policing the cropland and the communes fell to the district warden (*Bannwart*);[7] guarding the communal woods to the forest warden (*Forstwart*); beating the bounds and reporting trespassers to the boundary guard (*Untergänger*); guarding against fire to the fire watch (*Feuerschauer*); and the general police of the village, especially at night, to the night watch (*Wächter*). The delegation of such tasks to specific magistrates did not, of course, weaken the principle of communal self-government, because all these offices were filled by action of the entire commune.

In addition to these officers, the commune also possessed—to use a modern expression—"employees," who were also appointed by the commune. Chief among them were the herdsmen (*Hirten*), who, depending on the commune's size, could be specialized as day or night herdsmen or as herders of cattle, horses, hogs, or sheep. There were often also a beadle (*Büttel*), who carried messages for the four or the village officials, and the watermen (*Wässerer*), who irrigated the meadows, a job which was sometimes surprisingly complicated. Each of these employees was appointed for a term, usually one year.

Over all the communal officials named stood the mayor (*Schultheiß* or *Schulze*), also called headman (*Ammann*) or guardian (*Vogt*).[8] Though always a member of the commune, he was frequently appointed by the local lord or the territorial prince, who at the very least retained the right to confirm his appointment. This reservation reveals the office's double character, since the mayor represented the commune to the seigneur or prince and at the same time represented the rulers' interests in the commune. He functioned as leader of the commune's assembly, its chief administrator, and president of the village court.

The village court's judges (*Schöffen, Richter, Urteiler*) were sometimes elected by the commune, sometimes chosen by the court itself through co-optation, and sometimes appointed jointly by the prince or seigneur and the commune. The office's functions, which were often less purely judicial than administrative, included the verification of land titles, preparation of land registers (*Urbare, Grundbücher*) and tax registers (*Zinsbücher*), authentication of legitimate or free birth, and other tasks. Within limits, the village court possessed undisputed civil and criminal jurisdiction over communal affairs, by virtue of which it could try and punish violators. Actionable violations included the damaging of common lands through overcultivation or excessive mowing and the disturbance of the village's peace by means of insults, fights, or bodily injuries. These fell under what at the time was called "low justice," whereas "high justice," the jurisdiction over such capital crimes as murder, robbery, and arson, was administered by a higher authority, normally the territorial ruler.

To sum up, the extent of peasant self-government in the German rural commune was very broad. Wherever individual and collective interests collided, the commune intervened to adjudicate between them by means of the institutions it had created. Agriculture and all the problems connected with it became and remained the basis of peasant self-government in the village.

The Commune as a Political Association

During the fifteenth century, villages added to their general competency the economic and social regulation that fell under the very broad category of law and order (*gute Polizei*). To exercise these functions, the commune created institutions that possessed legislative power to command and forbid and judicial power to prosecute and punish violators.

This analysis fits only the fully developed commune, and there were naturally various degrees of autonomy and hence of self-government. We may nonetheless assume that rural communes of this type existed all over central Europe, where they belonged to the normal constitutional structures of the German territories until around 1800, when premodern society based on orders (*Ständegesellschaft*) came to an end.

We can summarize the rural communes' significance as follows. First, the village assumed elementary governmental (*staatlich*) tasks, such as guaranteeing justice and keeping the peace by means of the communal assembly's legislative authority and through powers delegated to the village administration and court. The general obligation of all villagers, however, to uphold law and order in the village at any price, with arms if necessary, was institutionalized to a lesser degree. It is important to recognize that this picture of rural self-government is not just a naive political idealization of the village, even granted that villages were not in full control of their lives. Within the hierarchical structure of the empire, of course, the guaranteeing of law and order was accomplished on different levels by means of diverse competencies. What the village lacked in truly political character—what distinguished it from, say, the large city—was its ability to protect itself against feuds and wars. The important thing, however, is not the degree to which the village assumed political functions, but the bare fact that it assumed them at all. The older legal historians recognized this when they ascribed to the village commune a function in public law.

Second, all of these village functions were exercised by members of the village commune. The degree to which a village's commune and its lord controlled the staffing of offices, which varied greatly by place and era, determined the relative weights of community and lordship in the village. The presence of lordship everywhere, however, should not obscure the fact that, once the village commune was constituted, the peasant was fully integrated into the political order. As Karl Siegfried Bader wrote, "we must not overestimate lordship's influence on everything that had to do with the agricultural system and the use of the soil, for in everyday life what is now—often for shock effect—called 'feudalism' reached far less deeply into peasant life than the one-sided picture transmitted by the sources makes it appear."[9]

Third, village and commune were not contraries but mutually supportive structures. The commune was the form in which the village participated politically in the society based on orders, but not all rural communes were based on villages. There were valley communes and rural communes without nucleated centers (*Landgerichte*), in all of which, despite dispersed settlement, the communal association undertook the same functions as the village commune did. Indeed, sometimes a village was established as the central place of such an association. Chronologically, such valley or other dispersed rural communes came together around the same time as the village communes by means of a process springing from similar changes in the forms of labor. Scholars employ the term "rural commune" (*Landgemeinde*) for all such forms.

The Development of Rural Communes

Having to this point looked at the village commune and the rural commune in a schematic way as models, we now turn to the actual historical forms that embodied the communal principle. We must continue to employ abstractions and models if we are not to become lost in the thicket of hundreds of individual examples. We will, therefore, sketch a picture of the commune more nuanced according to time and place.

Chronology of the Rural Commune

In order to frame the investigation properly, we must keep two basic facts in mind. First, seigneurial lordship and the state depended usually, sometimes exclusively, on the fruits of agriculture, in the productivity of which no major improvements occurred during the entire later Middle Ages and early mod-

The Commune as a Political Association

ern era. Ignoring variations in harvests, therefore, the gross social product of agriculture remained constant. Second, the lords and the state nevertheless faced constantly rising financial needs to expand the size of their administrative apparatus, to support the mounting costs (especially in the Renaissance era) of palaces and festivals, and to pay for their wars. Necessarily, therefore, rural society, in proportion to the state's financial dependence on agriculture, had to finance an ever more expensive government. This mounting burden obviously had an important impact on agriculture and rural society, that is, on the village and its commune.

An attempt to construct a chronology of the commune must begin with the emergence of the state—especially the territorial principality, since the rural commune had little or no direct connection to the empire[10]—as a dynamic factor in German history. This process may be conceived in two successive stages: the formation of territorial sovereignty and the age of absolutism. We know that the construction of territorial sovereignty in the fifteenth and sixteenth centuries involved both external demarcation of a territory against its neighbors and the internal consolidation of its governance. This process left untouched the rights of the inferior magistrates or intermediate authorities, such as the estates, abbeys, seigneuries, urban magistracies, and rural communes, although all of these became more subordinate to the territory and its prince. The second concept, absolutism, applies in Germany during the late seventeenth century and all of the eighteenth century to a form of government in exclusively princely hands, which deliberately and progressively curtailed the powers of the intermediate authorities, at least insofar as their authority rested on their own rights and was not derived exclusively from the state. These two stages of state development also altered the appearance of the commune.

If we assume that the ruler's interest in agriculture was primarily fiscal, we might expect him to have tried to increase his authority first where the yields were relatively high and the legal barriers relatively weak. This explains why, from the fifteenth century on, the ruler invaded the village and the commune through their commons. Beginning in the fifteenth and increasingly in the sixteenth century, economic recovery gave the woods and the pasture comprising the commons a new and enhanced economic significance.

The Commune as a Political Association

This was true of woodlands because timber, the most important raw material of the later Middle Ages and the early modern era, was becoming scarce; it was true also of pasture, however, because pasture formed the indispensable basis for the expansion of textile production, based on sheep-raising. Wherever the ruler and the villagers shared the commons, the ruler might try to secure a larger share of its use.

One means of gaining a stronger grip on the woodlands was the ruler's authority over the forest (*Forstbann*), though this originally extended to the forests alone and not to the communal woods. The exercise of this authority might promote a rational exploitation of the forests, and it normally did not ban the peasants from taking building timber, firewood, and fencing material from the forest, or from grazing their livestock there, especially their hogs. The sharp rise in sixteenth-century lumber prices encouraged the lords of the forests to use their rights selfishly and, in extreme cases, either to exclude the peasants from the forests altogether or to extract new fees for their use.

The lord's economic interest in the pastures was also connected with sheep-raising, which was becoming more profitable in Germany because of increasing meat shortages. New incomes could also be raised from the commons by leasing them as lots for building houses. The legal basis of the lords' privatization of the pastures was their general authority to command (*Bangewalt*), though in this case its use violated custom and was therefore illegal. The lord's authority over the forest and his power to regulate were extended to the communal woods, which was brought under the same regime as his own forests, though the peasants could not be prevented from using their own woods.

In short, during the fifteenth and sixteenth centuries the rulers acquired property rights in the commons, and the village commons was gradually brought under the princes' forest administrators. For the village and its commune, this meant the loss of one of its three component parts, the commons.

Wherever the state brought the commons under its own legislative authority and sought to incorporate it into a forest administration, it did so in a way that promoted the uniformity of territorial law. Laws regulating use of forests are found in the comprehensive forest ordinances that appeared in nearly all German territories around 1500. They aimed to rationalize forest use for fiscal ends and thus contained no recognition of local customs with respect to use of the forests. The only discernible exception respected the nobles' passion for hunting and sometimes allowed them to overstock the forests with wild game. Behind the legal unification lay the more general principle of eliminating highly variable local customs in favor of a uniform territorial law. The logic of this principle called for leveling the village's laws, which had grown out of their communal lawmaking activities and customs, and replacing them with a territorial code of law. The stages of this process can be documented for Swabia, where between 1500 and 1600 divergent village codes were superseded by a territorial village code that was later replaced by a territorial code. The territorial village code thus formed the intermediate step between the local law of the village codes and the territorial code valid for the entire land. Although the prince issued this transitional law separately for each village, every version of it possessed the same content.

Such village ordinances issued by rulers regulated the villages courts' composition and procedure, the criminal law and its fines, and the maintenance of law and order (*Polizei*). These steps opened decisive breaches in communal autonomy. Judicial procedure, for example, was made to conform increasingly to Roman legal procedure, with inevitable consequences: written procedure tended to replace oral procedure; representation by lawyers tended to replace face-to-face confrontations of the parties; and judgments tended to be handed down by educated presiding judges based on their study of written law. The judges (*Urteiler, Schöffen*) of the village courts could thereby be reduced to mere figureheads. The codification of criminal law and the introduction of schedules of fines truncated the old law-speaking function of the village court and reduced it to a mere confirmation of the judgment and sentence. Finally, new police laws deprived the Four and other communal officers of the power to tailor the stipulations of, for example, laws regulating manufactures, to local village needs.

In these ways, the development of territorial sovereignty curtailed the resources of local rural society by moving the commons under state control and by restricting the competency of the village commune both in the management of the commons, which came under the ruler's regime, and in legislative and judicial activity. Slowly but relentlessly, the expansive territorial legislation pressed against the borders of villages' self-government.

This does not mean, however, that the commune was simply reduced to an inferior unit of the state's superior government, something that happened only later—and then not everywhere—during the age of absolutism. The absolutist states systematically suppressed the old corporate rights and parliamentary institutions and treated subjects as children who had to be ruled for their own good. How this worked out in practice is clear from the experience of Austria, whose enlightened absolutist rulers commonly worked through the village priest to achieve their ends. In addition to his religious duties, the pastor was charged with organizing relief for the poor, promoting sanitation, and transmitting ideas about agricultural improvements. "The ideal late eighteenth-century pastor," it has been said, "was a 'father of the commune,' to whose tasks belong not only the cure of souls and education but also custody of the common weal of all those entrusted to him. This concept built very heavily on patriarchal relations of dependence, in which little place remained for an associative or communal element."[11]

To sum up, there was a correlation between the progressive intensification of the state's powers and the progressive shrinkage of the realm of communal autonomy. This conclusion needs nonetheless to be qualified by recognizing that the empire's various territories underwent this process in very different ways, so that we may speak here only of a general tendency. Further, we may not infer from it that by the end of the eighteenth century the communal culture of village life had everywhere died out. Indeed, we gain a deeper insight into the process only by examining some regional variations.

Geography of the Rural Commune

The rural commune possessing political functions was not limited to a single region. In fact, it can be shown that there were no major differences in this respect between old settled and newly settled lands, for the communal forms developed in the empire's western zones were transplanted to

The Commune as a Political Association

Transelbia during the great medieval colonization of the east, and in Saxony and Brandenburg the village exercised the same functions as it did in the Rhineland and in southwestern Germany.[12] This explains the similarity of fourteenth-century communal forms in widely separated parts of the empire, which allows us to speak of a common type of the village commune.

Certainly, over the succeeding centuries uniformity of this picture rapidly dissolved. In the Mark Brandenburg, for example, the village was stripped of its political functions before 1500. One peculiarity of the village constitution in fourteenth-century Brandenburg had been the tenured mayor (*Lehnschulze*), who held the office in hereditary tenure from his lord. As long as the ruling margrave was Brandenburg's premier authority, this office and the village constitution remained closely tied to the state. This situation began to change, however, when the nobles, called here "Junkers," began to gain control of the principality at the margrave's expense. He often obtained the nobles' consent to taxes by surrendering to them his own princely rights, including his jurisdiction over the village mayors' hereditary offices. In many cases, too, the same financial troubles that forced the margrave to ask his territorial estates for taxes led him to sell his own lands to nobles, who acquired thereby the margrave's jurisdiction over the mayoral offices and thus direct rule over the farmers. As the mayors' hereditary rights lapsed through deaths or were repurchased, they were replaced by mayors installed at will. These *Setzschulzen* were considerably more dependent on the noble lord, and sometimes the lord himself assumed this office. One gets a clearer picture of this transformation of ruler's rights by considering the 498 villages in Brandenburg that had once belonged to the margravial domain in the districts of Teltow, Barnim, Havelland, and Zauche. By 1375 only 28 remained in the elector-margrave's hands.[13] According to one authority, "as possessors of patrimonial jurisdiction, in the end the villages' noble lords united all rights of a landlord and judicial lord with the executive powers of a lord of the manor (*Gutsherr*)."[14] The village, in short, had lost its political functions.

Apparently, by 1500 Saxony had undergone a similar process, though the individual stages cannot be so well documented as in Brandenburg. In late medieval Saxony, the village lost "its criminal and civil jurisdiction, its entire voluntary (i.e., nonmanorial) jurisdiction, and its administrative authority" to the lord of the manor (*Gutsherr*). It thereby lost all competencies that "were connected with relations of public law."[15] Karlheinz Blaschke has described this process as a disfranchisement (*Entmündigung*) of the village commune. Eventually, this change meant that the roles once performed by village judges were transferred to university-trained jurists. The old village jurors (*Schöffen*) were reduced to mere figureheads or were simply abolished; the local judge was allowed to hold only the preliminary hearing; and judgments were passed by learned jurists in the lord's chancellery (plate 2).

These developments found in Brandenburg and Saxony apply as well to the other eastern territories. Between the fourteenth and the eighteenth century the noble estate owners (Junkers) legally acquired or usurped the rights of high and low justice, including the executive powers, that formed the content of traditional patrimonial authority. For the village this meant that all its old political and communal functions migrated into the Junker's chancellery and that consequently the village decayed into a purely social and economic unit.

Broadly viewed, developments in the empire's western regions resembled those in the east, although here the invasion of communal rights occurred on a significantly less drastic scale. Indeed, one can speak of invasions only during the age of absolutism, which as a rule came to the small western territories later—about the mid–eighteenth century—than they came to the east. Of the relatively few studies of rural communes in the early modern era, all document this change. In the western Austrian lands, for example, the communal associations and other parliamentary and corporate institutions (towns, provincial estates) retained their full powers until the administrative reforms of Maria Theresia (r. 1740–80) and Joseph II (r. 1765–90).[16]

More representative, probably, were relations in one of the lesser principalities, Nassau-Saarbrücken, where the state's domination of the village commune began in 1737. Its consequence was that "princely legislation in the form of village codes replaced the communal ordinances created by the vil-

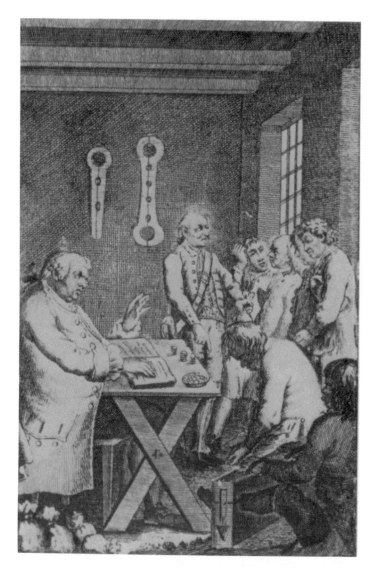

Plate 2. The exercise of low jurisdiction in southeastern Germany. From S. Rottmanner, *Unterricht eines alten Beamten an junge Beamte, Kandidaten und Praktikanten*, vol. 1 (Linz, 1783), title page.

lage associations."[17] Further, the princely regime established its right "to participate in filling communal offices," a right that was extended in 1778 to village offices in the stricter sense, such as the head of the local court (*Heimmeier*) and the field wardens (*Flurschütze*). The *Heimmeier*, formerly installed by the village itself as president of the village court, was replaced by a president who was both installed by and responsible to the state.

In the empire's western regions, therefore, the communes defended their old positions more vigorously than did their counterparts in the east, though they also stood under much weaker pressure from the rulers. This can be documented by an example from Swabia, where a local lord complained that the farmers "don't bring their quarrels and disputes before their lord, because they want to have everything heard and decided by their own stupid farmers' court."[18]

Although such sparse evidence must be used cautiously, it seems to support an argument for significant differences between communal constitutions in the eastern and western zones of the empire. So does the existence of transitional forms that are found in the central German region lying between these zones. The thesis grows stronger as we move from description to interpretation. A glance at the eastern regions suggests the incompatibility of autonomous village communes with a strong nobility, and we can argue that the destruction of the villages' autonomy or semiautonomy resulted from the transition to the Transelbian system of consolidated estates (*Gutsherrschaften*).[19] This shift transformed formerly free farmers into hereditary servile dependents by requiring that they work several days of unpaid labor each week and by forcing their children to work as laborers on the noble's estate—a de facto retrogression of the farmers to the unfree status that had been characteristic of the manorial system. We find such developments not only in Brandenburg and Saxony, but also in Lusatia, Bohemia, and large parts of Austria. Since these were all territories in which the nobles were numerous and powerful, we must conclude that feudalism, defined as noble lordship over dependent peasants, tended to maintain the subjects in an unfree status, to control their labor and its fruits, and thus to preserve them in a condition of political immaturity.

This argument is bolstered by a look at the analogous social and political structures in the empire's western regions. Here the evidence supports the correlative thesis that strongly developed communal autonomy corresponds to relatively weak noble lordship. The rural nobles of the west enjoyed neither the economic role of estate owner in the eastern sense nor the political role of judicial lord, which the eastern nobles also possessed. This has been well demonstrated for the Electorate of Trier and for the Duchy of Württemberg, both relatively large western territories. The only surviving western social group that resembled the eastern Junkers—untitled noble lords—was the free imperial knights. How unimportant they were is suggested by two figures: in the eighteenth century the entire empire contained only 1,600 estates of free imperial knights, whereas Bavaria alone contained 1,400 noble and clerical estates (*Hofmarken*), many of which were as extensive and as legally well endowed as those of an imperial knight.

The contrast between east and west rests on changes that had taken place since the fourteenth century, when noble families of knightly rank were certainly at least as numerous in the western regions of the empire as in the eastern. Their rapid decline in the west can be attributed chiefly to the late medieval agricultural depression, which drove noble incomes below subsistence levels. The nobles sought compensation either by degenerating into robber knights or by becoming ruinously indebted to urban lenders in order to maintain their traditional lifestyle. The chief beneficiaries of these changes were the free cities, for it was only in the classic "noble landscapes of Swabia, Franconia, and the Upper and Middle Rhine that the late medieval imperial free cities were able to accumulate significant territories of their own, often at noble expense."[20] The larger ones—Ulm, Nuremberg, and Strasbourg—each came to rule over no fewer than a hundred villages. In the empire's eastern lands, by contrast, the nobles, imitating the Teutonic Knights, survived the agricultural depression by supplying the major grain markets in heavily urbanized Flanders and grain-importing England, markets that could be reached by the relatively inexpensive water routes along the Oder and Vistula Rivers and the Baltic and North Seas. Furthermore, in the markedly less densely urbanized east, where the nobles were not so directly challenged by prosperous merchants and artisans, they were able to restrain their lifestyles within more modest bounds than could their western counterparts.

Variation in urban density offers another reason for the divergent fates of western and eastern rural communes. In the west the territorial states did not have to cover their needs from agriculture alone, as they did in the east, and they benefited by means of taxes and tolls from urban economic growth in southern Germany and the Middle and Lower Rhine Valley. Already by the fourteenth century, the elector of Cologne was drawing about three-quarters of his income from tolls and taxes. In Bavaria around 1500, by contrast, just under half of the state's income still came from the ducal domain, even though the dukes' land register included less than 10 percent of the arable land in Bavaria. Socioeconomic conditions in the west led to a tighter integration of the burghers into the territorial structure than was the case in the eastern and southeastern German territories. The provincial parliaments of Brandenburg and Austria were dominated by nobles, whereas those of Württemberg and Electoral Trier were dominated by the towns. In the west the leading posts in territorial administrations were filled by burghers, in the east by nobles.

The upshot of these different patterns of development was that in the empire's western territories the state depended less on the productivity of agriculture and, though at root still feudal, entered into a symbiotic financial relationship with the city and its burghers. This may explain why in the west the state's pressure on the village, which was constituted in a way similar to the city, was not as great as in the east.

One final observation helps to round out the contrast between east and west. Until the rise of absolutism after 1650, the German territorial state was equipped with a weakly articulated and poorly staffed bureaucracy. Territorial administrations had grown steadily from the fifteenth century onward, but before 1650 their officials did not assume, in most cases, the lowest levels of justice and administration. At best, the territorial state constructed an apparatus on the level of the district (*Amt*), a political unit about the size of a modern *Kreis*, which was very modestly equipped with personnel: normally one district official (*Amtmann*) and a secretary.[21] The state was thus forced to delegate the exercise of its powers, in the east overwhelmingly to the nobles in the form of patrimonial courts, in the west to the communes of all kinds.

A Comparison of Rural and Urban Communes

We have several times referred to the comparability between the village and the town; we therefore need to establish their common constitutional principles. Observations of the close connection between town and village began with Georg Ludwig Maurer (1790–1872), a nineteenth-century Bavarian jurist and historian. The subsequent separation, however, of scholarly research into urban history and agrarian history has resulted in the connections between them not being subjected to empirical verification or critique since Maurer's day. Indeed, the contrary is rather the case, since researchers, with a few exceptions, have so concentrated on either urban or agrarian history that they have ignored the common features of village and town. There have been a few exceptions. Georg von Below (1858–1927) and Barthel Huppertz, who studied particular regions of the Holy Roman Empire, tried to pursue Maurer's initial argument, and more recently Karl Siegfried Bader used his mastery of Swiss and Swabian sources to demand a serious investigation of the common structural features of village and town. "One of the stubbornly repeated errors of urban historians," he wrote, "has been to concentrate chiefly on the large, economically most important cities, while they have simultaneously either ignored the countless small urban settlements or at least badly underestimated their significance for the entire problem of medieval" and, one might add, early modern "urban development. Precisely in the small and tiny towns, whose legal standing as cities is undeniable, there persisted many points of contact and similarities between town and village."[22] Bader's scholarly judgment recapitulates the medieval legal adage, "Nothing more than a wall separates the burgher from the peasant."[23]

We must remind ourselves that the large cities—Cologne, Nuremberg, Augsburg, and Strasbourg—cannot be considered representative of all cities. It has been calculated that the fifteenth-century empire contained 3,000 cities, of which 2,800 housed between 100 and 1,000 residents, so that more than

90 percent of the towns must be reckoned as small or even minuscule towns (*Kleinstädte*). They were scarcely larger than villages, many of which contained some hundreds of persons. Around 1500, for example, about half the villages belonging to the Abbey of Ottobeuren in Swabia contained between 250 and 500 inhabitants. We must remember, too, that the empire's village communes and urban communes developed in tandem since the thirteenth century, and that before 1200 there had been only about 50 cities in Germany. It can also be shown that in central and northern Germany the typical city only gradually differentiated itself from the typical village. Furthermore, Franz Steinbach (1895–1964) demonstrated that in the Rhineland and on the Middle and Lower Rhine, "the laws on communal constitutions prescribe no difference between urban and rural communes."[24]

Establishing the comparability of city and village has been chiefly the achievement of Karl Siegfried Bader. He has done so both negatively by downplaying the significance of the city's walls, long regarded as a decisive difference, and positively by noting common structural principles. Even today, the traveler through Franconia, the Palatinate, or Alsace has difficulty distinguishing city from village by outward appearances, since villages also commonly have walls. Historical research confirms this impression, showing that the existence of a wall is not a reliable criterion for distinguishing city from village. During the later Middle Ages and into the early modern era, such cities as Coblenz, Wetzlar, Meschde, and Tondern were fortified only with palisades that scarcely differed from village fences, whereas there are villages whose walls date from the fifteenth and sixteenth centuries.

The structural similarities, which are more important and more informative, concern the comparability of village and urban residential and economic spaces. The residential spaces of village and city were divided into farmsteads (*Hofstätte*) or town sites, the only places on which construction was allowed. Only the possessor of such a residence could use the common properties, which were exactly comparable in village and town. The residential area of village or city was also a specially protected zone of peace and peacekeeping, a feature that usually distinguished urban law from territorial and land laws, though village law, too, often defined the village as a special legal zone.

Based on functional criteria, town life and village life display a parallel development from first to last: communal assemblies, legislative authority, and judicial powers are just some of the institutions and competencies that occur in both milieus. Did burghers think themselves closer to peasants than to princes? Or is it significant that civic buildings in the Renaissance style employed the peasant, but not the noble, as a symbol (plate 3)?

We must nevertheless acknowledge certain differences between town and village. There is no rural equivalent, for example, of the urban sworn association (*coniuratio*), though such associations were often also lacking in towns that grew up around castles and markets during the thirteenth and fourteenth centuries. But on the whole, town and village display more common features than differences. Urban liberty, which in the form of the legal proverb, "town air makes you free," often cited as an essential urban characteristic, did not really define a great difference. If, following Karl Bosl, we understand the medieval concept of liberty correctly as the freedom to dispose of one's own labor, then this applied equally to the peasants in the era after the dissolution of the manor. And by the sixteenth century, even serfdom, which even today is often held to have been significant for the peasants, was not an important criterion of legal or social differentiation.

Did the Commune Threaten the Feudal State?

In 1407 the bishops of Augsburg and Constance, the duke of Teck, seven counts, and eighty-six nobles formed an alliance to assure that "we all, individually and severally, secure aid and advice in the best and most expeditious way against the peasants of Appenzell and all of those allied to them." This sworn alliance, which gave birth to the Society of Saint George's Shield, a forerunner of the Swabian League (est. 1488), arose against the threat which the Appenzellers, who were subjects of the Imperial Abbey of Saint Gall, were posing to the feudal powers in the regions around Lake Constance. Their alliance with their neighbors, called the League above the Lake, stretched from the Graubünden to the northern bank of Lake Constance and from the Arlberg to the eastern boundary of the Swiss Confederacy. Modeled on the confederacy, this alliance was also based on rural and urban communes, and, like the confederacy, it excluded the ruling nobles and

Plate 3. Hans Holbein's sketch for a mural on the house called "Zum Tanz" in Basel. (Copper plate engraving, water color in the Staatliche Museen zu Berlin, Preussischer Kulturbesitz, KdZ3104; photograph by Jörg P. Anders)

prelates. It is altogether probable that in forming the Society of Saint George's Shield, the Swabian nobles aimed to oppose a political union that negated in principle their feudal forms of governance. The nobles' reaction illustrates the incompatibility of feudal and communal principles, and the documented behavior of the Habsburgs and their noble clientele toward the Swiss strengthens this impression of antagonism. Ever since the Swiss defeat of the Habsburgs near Morgarten in 1315, the Austrian and Swabian nobles had developed a fear of the Swiss that can only be called pathological. In the Habsburg and neighboring regions during the later Middle Ages and beyond, the nobles feared the rise of a "new Switzerland." The image served to demonize any alternative principle to feudalism.

The principle of inequality lay at the basis of the feudal order. This is shown by many sources, most clearly perhaps in the great thirteenth-century lawbooks called the *Sachsenspiegel* and the *Schwabenspiegel*. They record the feudal military hierarchy (*Heerschildordmung*), which divided the feudality into six or seven ranks—king, ecclesiastical princes, lay princes, upper nobility, middle nobility, and minsterials and others eligible for knighthood. The ranks enjoyed different political rights and represented a relatively strict system of legal differences.

The principle of the equality of full members, by contrast, lay at the heart of the communal order. To the degree that communal membership in town and village was attached to the possession of a residence, only residents (*Häuser*) enjoyed political rights. This meant in practice that only male heads of household—the householders—exercised political rights within the commune. Commune and householders formed the structural principles of urban and rural society in the Holy Roman Empire. In practice, the householders made up hardly more than 20 percent of the population, so that the terminology used by the classical Aristotelian doctrine of the forms of state is more a hindrance than a help to comprehension. Above all, the recent literature agrees in holding that we should avoid speaking of the commune in terms of "democracy."

Just as feudalism sought to defend itself against the commune and to restrict the space of the commune, so the commune also tended to exclusivity in the form of political autonomy. If one follows the account of Franz

Steinbach, the commune thus became a threat to the feudal order, whereas social historians influenced by Otto Brunner (1898–1982) tend to present the relations between burghers and nobles in terms of harmony rather than dissonance.

The communal principle's threat to the feudal order can be seen with special clarity in the imperial free cities, whether of episcopal or royal origin. The episcopal cities' constitutions derived their authority from the bishop as lord of the city, from the king or his vicar (*Vogt* or *Landvogt*), and from the urban commune. Briefly stated, the urban commune's progress toward autonomy began when the urban commune and the royal protector pruned back the bishop's powers, an act symbolized by the removal of the bishop's residence from his cathedral city: from Augsburg to Dillingen, from Strasbourg to Saverne, and from Constance to Meersburg. The second phase saw the commune's absorption of the episcopal governor's rights. In royal cities, especially those founded by the Hohenstaufen dynasty, the process of communal emancipation can be seen clearly in the appointment and function of the officer called the mayor (*Ammann*). As the central administrative and judicial figure, the mayor was originally appointed by the king or his governor (*Landvogt*). Then the commune gained a right to participate in the mayor's selection. Finally, the commune secured the right to elect him and enhanced his jurisdiction through the acquisition of rights of high justice. These, if not the only processes involved, were some of the decisive stages on the cities' path to becoming direct subjects of the empire (*reichsunmittelbar*).[25] The commune's efforts to expand step-by-step the radius of its autonomy are shown by the concurrent processes of endowing the city with its own law, of exempting it from foreign courts, and of eliminating serfdom from the city. At the end of this development, the former episcopal and royal cities attained a legal position within the association of imperial estates that allowed the lordship of territories and the governance of cities to be conceived as functionally analogous to each other. Although it could be objected that only about 2 percent of all fifteenth-century cities in the empire attained this level of political autonomy, this objection cannot obscure the efforts of the communally organized city to extricate itself from the feudal order. And if this effort succeeded only rarely and often incompletely, it did so because of factors—temporally and spatially varied political constellations and economic processes—that are not at issue here. It suffices here to observe that the reciprocal relationship of economic and political power was such that the urban commune's political freedom of action expanded with the city's economic strength and the ruler's political weakness. The emancipation of the imperial cities during the later Middle Ages empirically confirms this observation.

This situation also explains why rural communes scarcely ever attained a comparable level of independence. The handful of imperial free villages aside, the degree to which a rural commune was incorporated into a territorial principality, and the fact that the late medieval and early modern territorial principality itself was striving for full statehood within the empire, made the rural commune's vantage point much less favorable than that of its urban counterpart. Nonetheless, there are examples of the parallel development of urban and rural communes. The political association of the Swiss Confederacy, to take one example, was based initially on autonomous rural communes, and the same was true in the neighboring land of Graubünden and, with qualifications, in Ditmarsh on the North Sea coast. In each case the decisive step was marked by the communalization of the protectorate (*Vogtei*), that is, by the integration of public law, state, and the ruler's functions into the commune. This process confirms once again the comparability of political emancipation in the city and on the land.

Where the desire to expand the commune's political zone of action could not secure for it imperial free status, it had to be satisfied within the existing statelike formation of the territorial state. This occurred by means of the integration of the communes into existing parliamentary corporations or by the creation of such corporations. Both developments depended on the same principle.

Chapter 2

Popular Representation in Parliamentary States

The concept of the territorial estate (*Landschaft*) has a double meaning. It means both the territory (*Land*) itself, which in the later Middle Ages and early modern era was synonymous with the territorial state, and it means the corporate parliamentary institutions as contrasted with the prince and his personal regime. The parliamentary state and the parliamentary ruler were thus complementary concepts and institutions.

This concept of a territorial parliamentary state applies only to the territorial principalities of the Holy Roman Empire, though the parliamentary phenomenon itself was known all over Europe. Established during the later Middle Ages, during the early modern era it intensified the bipolar character of the state, so that the monarchical principle (emperor, king, prince) and the associative principle (Imperial Diet, parliaments, territorial diets) complemented one another. The associative principle usually took the form of parliamentary estates made up of the territory's nobles, prelates, and towns, who demanded and acquired rights in the state's entire field of action—legislation, administration, and defense. For this reason we must dispense with the simple Aristotelian classification of state forms—monarchy, aristocracy, and polity—and recognize the parliamentary state (*Ständestaat*) as the dominant form of state in Europe during the ancien régime. Swiss historian Werner Näf (1894–1959) provided the classic constitutional formula for such states: "Prince and territory stand alongside one another, each with its own rights, the two with equal rights, and from this double source flows the state's power. Administrative, legislative, and fiscal practice developed under the oversight of and via the collaboration of prince and estates."[1]

In Germany this parliamentary principle unfolded on two levels: on the imperial level in the dualistic collaboration of emperor and Imperial Diet (*Kaiser und Reichstag*); and on the territorial level in that of territorial prince and territorial parliament (*Landesfürst und Landtag*). At first glance, the Imperial Diet and the territorial parliaments look very different, but we may well ask whether they do not represent two developments of the same basic structure. We must emphasize, with reference to the problem dealt with in this book, that in general on the imperial level the communal principle was represented only by the imperial free cities, not by rural communes. Even here are exceptions, since Schwyz and Ditmarsh received invitations to attend Imperial Diets, and some communal associations, such as the Free Folk on the Leutkirch Moor, paid their share of the taxes voted by the diet, which suggests that they were indeed represented, perhaps by a nearby free city. There is no simple explanation for the failure of these free rural associations to become full imperial estates. The Swiss Confederacy split away from the empire; Ditmarsh was conquered and subjected to princely rule; and the free villages of the Leutkirch Moor became Habsburg subjects through the institution of mortgage.

The question of how the communal principle was integrated, sometimes forcibly, into the state can best be studied empirically in the territorial principalities. Here the institutional framework was the territorial parliament (*Landschaft*), which Otto Brunner described definitively. He distinguished three types of territorial parliaments or estates (*Landschaften*), corresponding roughly to the fourteenth, fifteenth, and sixteenth centuries. In the fourteenth century and earlier, *Landschaft* was composed of the territorial estates and their territorial prince; in the fifteenth century it comprised the estates alone; and from the sixteenth century onward the parliamentary estates were either a privileged territorial corporation or, as in the Netherlands, lords of the land. The polarity of prince and estates was already formulated in the regional legal codes (*Landrechte*) of the High Middle Ages, which bound a prince and his people together and created an authority over institutions and individuals. This regional law comprised both the ruler's sovereign rights and the estates' privileges. The capacity of the existing legal order to adapt further via agreement among all parties was expressed in the formulas, found in thousands of medieval charters, that the estates were obliged to supply "advice and aid" (*Rat und Hilfe*), while the lord provided them with "defense and protection" (*Schutz und Schirm*). This legal concept acquired ethical expression in the oath of loyalty (*Huldigungseid*), which indicates that the political order was held to be sacred.

Gradually, joint military and judicial actions of lord and territory were superseded by a process of dealing with one another, which was institutionalized in the form of territorial parliaments (*Landtage*). This process, combined with the replacement of a polarized structure by a dualistic one, arose from the territorial princes' efforts to monopolize the law and to promote the idea of positive legislation at the expense of the older procedure of merely finding the law. From this process sprang an unavoidable antagonism between princely and parliamentary sovereignty, the theoretical poles of which were formulated respectively by Jean Bodin (1530–1596) and Johannes Althusius (1557–1638).

The estates incorporated into territorial parliaments rested on the unit of the household. For Otto Brunner, membership in the territory (*Landschaft*) belonged to every inhabitant who possessed a house. The householder exercised lordship, whether in a noble household or in one analogously conceived, such as a monastery possessing rights of immunity. This is why in the early days the territorial parliaments did not include the princes' own domains, whose people belonged to the ruler's "house," for example the House of Austria. Accepting this explanation nonetheless creates difficulties concerning the parliamentary membership of cities, which also belonged to the princely domain. Evidently they outgrew that status when they assumed functions analogous to those of the noble household. Yet, taking the "noble household," which is the basis of Brunner's theory, as the standard requires a somewhat forced explanation for the cities' representation in the territorial parliaments.

Michael Mitterauer has taken the matter further with reference to the literature on estates. Looking at Europe as a whole, he concludes that the definitive marks of a true estate are a relationship to the ruler and the possession of "independent rights of lordship," which could be personal, as with nobles, bishops, and prelates, or collective. Among the latter, collective, estates belong the urban and rural communes. Mitterauer places them under the category of the "autonomous urban and rural commune," by which he means what we are calling "the commune having political functions." Mitterauer writes that "Simplified as a model, the structure of medieval estates presents a matrix of noble and ecclesiastical householders, on the one hand, and urban and rural communal associations, on the other. The urban communes were also composed of householders, who participated, either directly or indirectly [i.e., through guilds], in the civic regimes. Further simplified, the same is true of the rural commune."[2]

Origins of Parliamentary States in the Empire

The origins of parliamentary constitutions in the German territories date back no earlier than the late thirteenth century in Brandenburg, Bavaria, and some other states, and no later than the early sixteenth century in the Prince-bishopric of Basel. They began earlier in the large territories and later in the small ones; in general, they were formed during the later Middle Ages.

Does this rough chronology suggest the reasons for their formation? To answer this we must begin with the idea that the formation of parliaments was an important political process, an explanation for which must lie in late medieval political developments. One decisive political change was the shift of governance from the empire to the territories in the later Middle Ages, when a weakened monarchy meant that the social problems of law and order had to be dealt with by lesser authorities, the territorial princes. The empire's loss of importance was thus balanced by the territories' gain in authority.

The process of disintegration at the empire's pinnacle corresponded to a similar process at its base, namely, the disintegration of the traditional agrarian order. This happened through two movements: the shift from the manorial community to the village, and the migration of artisanal production and exchange from the countryside into the city. These changes created economic and social problems that, where they were not addressed by communes, created a pressure "from below" for law and order, thus enhancing the territorial principality's importance. This demand for more effective government expressed the need for both a defined boundary of jurisdiction and an administrative apparatus to handle the problems in a legitimate and effective way. Such a redefinition of jurisdictions necessarily violated the traditional practice of law, whereas the new administrative organs did the same in the area of finance. From the moment of its inception, therefore, the territorial state faced a pressing need for legal unification on a territorial basis and for taxes to cover financial burdens that exceeded the prince's personal means. According to traditional ways of thinking, this required innovations that needed the consent of the governed. Since the changes affected territorial, urban, and village law, and since the new taxation burdened the gross social product, those who were affected and whose consent was therefore needed included the nobles, prelates, burghers, and peasants. This connection was recognized at the time, both in the empire and in the rest of Europe. As contemporary legal thinking had it, "What touches all must be judged by all" (*Quod omnes tangit ab omnibus approbari debet*).[3] Other explanations, such as the widespread notion that the parliaments were organized only for taxation, are inadequate because they ignore other fundamental duties and functions of the parliaments.

Parliamentary Integration and Peasant Estates

For about the last hundred years it has been recognized that peasants—or more accurately, rural communes—enjoyed widespread political representation in early modern German territories. We can no longer be satisfied by the older, trivializing explanation, advanced by Hermann Aubin, that the political rights of the Frisians and the Swiss arose from their peculiar natural environments. On the contrary, the peasants' role in the state constitutions of diverse territories—such as the prince-bishoprics of Salzburg and Basel, the counties of Tyrol and Frisia, and the prince-abbeys of Kempten and Ochsenhausen—forces us to seek different reasons for that role. We should also ask why historians have ignored this phenomenon for so long.

Let us begin with the second point. For a long time, historians associated the concept of territorial parliaments with the notion of "ruling estates"— the nobles and the clergy. This agreed with the sociological and historical concepts advanced by Max Weber, who defined an "estate" (*Stand*) as "a plurality of persons who, within a larger group, successfully claim a) a special social esteem, and possibly also b) status monopolies." He added that estates were distinguished from one another by such characteristics as lifestyle, formal education, and prestige associated with descent or occupation. These characteristics were expressed in rights of endogamy (*connubium*), commensalism, and in the "monopolistic appropriation of privileged modes of acquisition or the abhorrence of certain kinds of acquisition."[4] So formulated, the definition can hardly be made to include peasants. To exclude them from the order of estates, however, as Weber implicitly does, prevents us from understanding the peasant's role as a political estate within his territory.

Two examples will help us see the principles that underlay the political representation of rural society: the County of Tyrol, a large "constituted"— that is, formally articulated—parliamentary state; and the Prince-abbey of Kempten, a small, "nonconstituted" state.[5] Then we can judge how applicable our findings are to other states.

Tyrol: A Constituted Parliamentary State

The Tyrolean parliament probably formed around 1300 as an outgrowth of the princely council and the comital court, which often met together at Meran. This fact has certain implications for the jurisdictions and composition of the first parliamentary bodies. We know of them from the decisions about these topics taken by such councils, whose chief concerns seem to have been rendering support for and advice to the prince and the administration of law. Nobles and at least some of the towns made up the "political," that is the represented, estates. The early parliamentary appearance of towns in this county may stem from the fact that in Tyrol the burghers of Meran staffed the prince's court of law (*Hofgericht*). During the first half of the fourteenth century, the circle of the represented expanded to include other towns and marketplaces. Finally, during the latter half of the century the Tyrolean rural districts (*Landgerichte*) were invited to attend, followed by the abbots of the nonimperial abbeys. By 1439 at the latest, the four-house Tyrolean parliament was fully formed. This parliamentary corporation (*Landschaft*) embraced, in contemporary language, "the notables and clergy, all prelates, abbots, provosts, and clerical folk, and the nobles, including all barons, knights, and squires, plus all the people of the towns, marketplaces, and rural districts and valleys of our county of Tyrol in the Etsch Valley, in the Inn Valley, also in the Val Sugana and in Ticino."[6] The register from 1468 lists fifty-three rural districts represented in the parliament, a number that, with occasional changes, remained stable down to the end of the parliamentary constitution.

The Tyrolean rural district (*Landgericht*) was a corporation functioning very much like a village commune, from which it was distinguished only by its dispersed membership, a difference easily explained by the natural environment and the resulting patterns of settlement. The rural district embraced those peasants who stood directly under the prince's jurisdiction, the relationship to which defined membership in the rural district. The tenants and judicial subjects of an abbey or lay seigneur were also organized into a seigneurial association (*Hofmark*), but, because such lordships had no parliamentary structures, their subjects' interests were represented by the abbot or lay lord.

Based on these facts we can say with certainty that one of the essential marks of membership in the parliamentary structure was a direct relationship to the prince, such as nobles, clergy, burghers, and peasants had. We must now turn to the organization and functions of this right to sit in the parliament.

Tyrol: Representation of the Rural Districts

In Tyrol the right to sit in parliament, which the prince's immediate subjects possessed, was embodied in the rural districts' parliamentary representation. The prince's call to assembly was directed to the rural districts; the district itself or a committee of its commune then empowered an envoy to represent the district, provided him with limited powers of decision, and charged him with presenting the district's grievances to the parliament. His credentials explained why more extensive demands by the prince to the parliament had to be referred for ratification to the whole district commune. This principle, which justified, announced, and executed the subjects' claim to base all political decision on a broad local consensus, naturally could weaken the parliament's operations to the point of total ineffectiveness. The need for consent to all decisions makes clear why the peasants sought to be included in the incorporated estates of the territories. The genuinely political character of the commune corresponded to its claim for representation in the decision-making bodies on a higher political level than its own. The truly political character of this claim is clear from the justification of the communal grievances, which today could be called the "right of petition."

What has been said of the rural districts was also true for the towns and marketplaces, so that various sectors of the Tyrolean common people developed political access on the basis of the same principles. The importance of their representation was symbolized by the equality of the four houses of the Tyrolean parliament—nobles, clergy, towns and marketplaces, and rural districts—which was replicated in the parliamentary committees. In the Large Committee of the parliament, the four houses normally possessed ten seats each; in the Small Committee of twenty-five seats, the two upper houses had a majority of one vote over the two lower ones.

The majority share of the towns and rural districts in these parliamentary bodies reflects the fact that, uniquely in the German-speaking territories, the Tyrolean peasants were sometimes accepted as the prince's sworn councilors. In 1440 the territorial parliament provided to his sworn council six nobles, six burghers, and six peasants; in 1487 there were still two burghers and two peasants among the sixteen councillors.

At the zenith of the Tyrolean parliamentary constitution during the fifteenth and early sixteenth centuries, the common people attained their greatest political significance. From the sixteenth century onward they were underrepresented in the territorial regime, and their participation in the Tyrolean parliament declined accordingly. Whereas in the fifteenth century the rural districts were represented in parliament overwhelmingly by peasants, by the eighteenth century this role lay in the hands of lawyers—a sign that the peasants, no longer understanding the processes of political decision-making, had allowed themselves to be marginalized in political life.

Tyrol: The Common Man's Parliamentary Role

Tyrolean parliamentary history displays the wide-reaching—if not always complete—congruence of interests among towns, villages, and valleys. A comparison of the grievances of the nobles and clergy, on the one side, and the towns and rural districts, on the other, reveals a clear division of interests. In general, in the most significant areas subject to parliamentary decisions—legislation, defense, and taxation—the combined interests of burghers and peasants repeatedly prevailed.

In legislation this predominance is already apparent in the ordinances for parts of the county issued in 1404, 1420, 1474, and 1489. These laws, which dealt mainly with agriculture, urban economies, and legal administration, owed their existence to burgher-peasant initiatives in parliament, and the princes and their counselors merely revised and occasionally supplemented the texts. This reveals clearly how the common people's parliamentary representation contributed to the solution of Tyrol's structural problems. Apparently, the weakly developed princely administration was incapable of diagnosing, much less confronting, such problems.

The great Tyrolean constitution of 1526 was the direct successor of these late medieval parliamentary ordinances. It underwent slight modifications in 1532 and revision and expansion in 1573, when it received the form it retained until well into the nineteenth century. This constitution of 1526, which reflects the grievance lists of ninety-six articles drafted at Meran and Innsbruck in 1525, in the midst of the great Peasants' War, is little more than a translation of the burghers' and peasants' demands into statutory law. Although the prince, Archduke Ferdinand, was able to prevent the realization of some truly revolutionary demands, such as the dissolution of monasteries and the political emasculation of the nobility, he could not refuse the other reforms his burghers and peasants demanded. Several improvements were made in the judicial administration, for example, that were favorable to popular interests: the payment of judges was shifted from a share of the fines to fixed salaries; advocates' fees were limited to one Bernese pound; and noble servitors and officials lost their legal immunities vis-à-vis the urban and rural courts. Other changes favorable to the peasants were made in the laws governing rural life, such as the stipulation that all lords must rent their lands on heritable leases (*Erbzinsrecht*), the form most favorable to the peasants. The transfer fine (*Ehrschatz*) was reduced from 10 percent of the holding's value to the merely symbolic level of a pound of pepper. Labor dues (*Roboten*) could be claimed only by lords who could document that the dues had existed continuously for more than fifty years, and the peasants received limited rights to hunt and to fish. Other changes promoted more secure food supplies and stricter price controls: the standardization of weights and measures, prohibitions of sales outside the official marketplaces and of the export of livestock, and the dissolution of the guild jurisdictions.

It is unnecessary to extend the history of this ordinance beyond 1526 because these provisions show sufficiently how this law met the demands of the burghers and the peasants. As with all other early modern legal codifications, of course, late medieval legal decisions crept into the law of 1526, but in Tyrol the popular influence on these older codes had already been quite strong. Indeed, one can say that the Tyrolean codification betrays a certain dominance of the towns' and rural districts' houses in the territorial parliament. This can be seen in the military organization and provisions for the county's defense. This sector gained its constitutional form from a law (*Landlibell*) of 1511, which remained in force until the end of the eighteenth century. The law had two principal parts. The first part concerned the territorial army. It divided the estates' share of the territorial militia, allotting 36 percent to the nobles and clergy, 48 percent to the towns and rural districts, and the balance, 16 percent, to the newly acquired lordships and districts of the Pustertal, Kitzbühl, Rattenberg, and Kufstein. Considering the modest aggregate size of the noble and monastic seigneuries in Tyrol, this law assessed them quite heavily, so heavily, indeed, that when they found themselves unable to fill their quotas from their own subjects, these lords had to recruit mercenaries from the towns and rural districts, a costly practice unknown in most territorial states.

While the Tyrolean parliament already had the right of consent to the size and costs of all defense measures, the law of 1511 fixed the estates' obligation to pay the territorial army at one month, at the end of which the prince had to assume paying the troops, as if they were mercenaries. In addition, the prince had to supply five hundred to six hundred cavalry at his own expense. These rules derived from older Tyrolean military traditions, according to which, as we know from the rural codes (*Weistümer*), burghers and peasants did not have to serve beyond the town's hinterland or beyond the rural district and could not be sent more than "one day's journey" from home. Such limitations made no sense, of course, once princely authority expanded and the county grew larger, and they later had to be adjusted to current conditions. Such an innovation required consent and came, therefore, before the Tyrolean parliament. This explains both the estates' right to be consulted about war and peace and the joint financial responsibility of prince and parliament for territorial defense.

From the sixteenth into the eighteenth century, the Tyrolean estates always paid close attention to military affairs, as is evidenced by the large number of ordinances about migration and defense. They were partly responsible for Tyrol's ability to construct an effective militia system, such as the kind Niccolò Machiavelli (1469–1527) recommended for all republics. In 1636, for example, Tyrol's militia enrolled up to eighty-four thousand men, who were trained on Sundays and holidays in a three-year rotation. In 1809, led by Andreas Hofer (1767–1810), this Tyrolean militia won a convincing victory over French and Bavarian troops.

The tax system, which developed along lines parallel to the military, was the second subject of the ordinance (*Landlibell*) of 1511. This law provided that the nobles and clergy should produce 36 percent of the total out of their own incomes. Their tax obligations dated to 1406, when the nobles' and monasteries' subjects had first been assessed. In 1468 the nobles and monasteries themselves had been assessed 10 percent on their incomes. This imposition of taxes on the upper estates, though rare, was not unique, and its coincidence with the rural districts' inclusion in the parliament is suggestive, though the evidence too sparse to connect the two facts as cause and effect.

Tyrol provides a clear example of how highly developed popular political rights could become, and it is particularly apt for showing the political potential of the burghers and peasants, if they represented their causes energetically enough. This political weight was not determined, as is often alleged, by purely environmental factors. A look at the Tyrolean constitution of 1526 suffices to show that.

Tyrolean parliamentary history provides a good vantage point for studying popular parliamentary representation in other large states having dualistic—that is, prince-and-parliament—constitutions. In the lands of the prince-archbishop of Salzburg, the parliamentary representation of the rural districts (*Gerichte*) was a consequence of the tax revolt of 1462. Other such cases are known, such as the Margraviate of Baden, where the estates' development may go back to the revolt called the Poor Conrad in 1514. We nevertheless cannot establish active resistance to authority as the cause of parliamentary representation of peasants, for the decisive factor was their own political interests.

The parliamentary representation of peasants is known in the Habsburg lands of Swabian Austria and Vorarlberg, the Prince-archbishopric of Salzburg and the Prince-bishopric of Basel, the Duchy of Württemberg, the

Margraviate of Baden, the Electorate of Trier, and the County of East Frisia, plus (but only briefly) the Rhine Palatinate. To all of these states the Tyrolean pattern applies: where the common man was integrated into the parliamentary system, his interests were more highly respected in territorial legislation than in territories were he lacked representation. This proposition can be tested by using the examples of Tyrol, Bavaria, Brandenburg, and East Frisia. In Brandenburg the noble-dominated parliament effectively protected the Junkers' economic and legal position against the prince's demands for taxes. The course of events was similar in Electoral Saxony, where in 1651 the parliament was forced to pass a law providing for labor services by tenants. This would have been unthinkable in a parliament in which rural communities were represented, and, in fact, no such law is found in any other territory. The communal element was very weak in Electoral Saxony's parliament, even though the princely domain—normally a main basis for such representation—was relatively large. This weakness is to be explained by the fact that in Saxony the urban and rural communes either never acquired or could not maintain political rights.

Wherever the common man was integrated into the parliamentary system, his financial obligations relative to the other estates were lower. Taxation followed the principle of the equality of the represented estates, to the disadvantage of the nobles and clergy and to the advantage of the burghers and peasants.

Political representation of the common man on the territorial level presupposed the transition from the medieval to the late medieval sociopolitical order, that is, from the manorial association to the neighborhood-oriented commune, with all of its aforementioned consequences. This change altered the political relationships, which had previously been exclusively vertical in nature. While during the High Middle Ages, the vassal's subjects had possessed no direct relationship to the territorial prince, the later Middle Ages witnessed the development of just such relationships (fig. 3).

Behind this change stood the formation of the commune possessed of political functions, which added a third factor, the commune, to the two earlier participants in government, the prince and his vassals. The peasants thus acquired by means of the commune a direct relationship to the territorial prince. Legally, this change meant a merger of two sharply distinct legal jurisdictions, territorial law and seigneurial law (fig. 4). Whereas during the High Middle Ages seigneurial law insulated the peasant from the sphere of territorial law, which pertained to the feudal elite alone, in the later Middle Ages seigneurial law was integrated into territorial law by means of the legal activities of urban and rural communes.

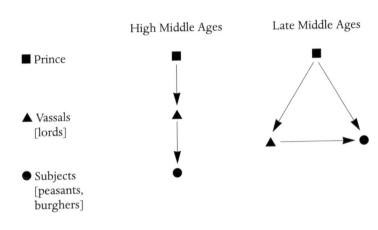

Fig. 3. The medieval parliamentary state.

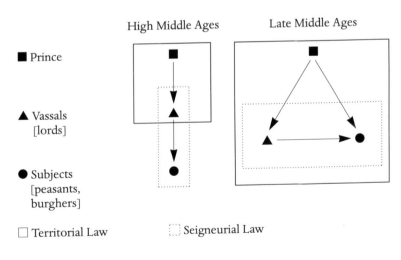

Fig. 4. Transformation of the parliamentary state.

If we connect these deductions to the well-known conclusions and theses of Otto Brunner, who held territorial law to be the foundation for creating estates, it becomes clear that the relative equality of vassals and commune and the integration of seigneurial law into territorial law forced the integration of the common man into the structure of the state by means of his communes (fig. 5).

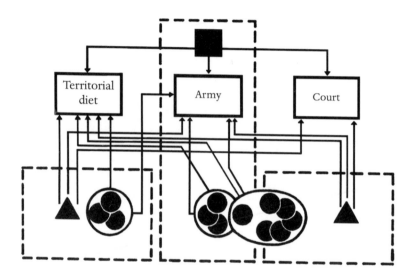

Fig. 5. The parliamentary state of the late Middle Ages and early modern period in Upper (southern) Germany. ■ = prince; ▲ = lord; ● = community (village, court, city)

The formation of the territorial parliament thus presupposed both the commune itself and the principles that lay at the foundations of both institutions. But do not misunderstand this process as a mechanically causal one: the will to realize these principles was needed to bring them into practice. This becomes clearer when we shift our intention to the small, nonconstituted parliamentary states.

The Abbey of Kempten: A Nonconstituted Parliamentary State

"Nonconstituted" refers to states that failed, whether because of their small size or for other reasons, to develop a dualistic government of prince-and-parliament by the fifteenth century. One such state was the Prince-abbey of Kempten, where the beginnings of the corporate parliamentary constitution (*Landschaft*) go back to the year 1491. The prince-abbot described the events thus:

> His Grace says that in the year 1491 around Saint Martin's Day (11 November), sixty men gathered secretly on the Wischberg, not far from the abbey, and bound themselves together by an oath, which they swore in common (*in der ainung*). They swore that what should happen to one should be the business of all, and each should protect, guard, and watch over the other. They set up a pike, and whoever wanted to join the union should walk under the pike. All did this and so were obliged and sworn to one another.
>
> Then the sworn men went to a neighboring parish, in the hope that they would also join the undertaking, and they went from place to place through My Gracious Lord's county, both the upland and the lowland districts. In each place they rang the church bell and forced many of those who gathered to join their union. They appointed and installed their own captains, just as the complaint charges, and assembled at Lubass in large numbers. There those who joined the union swore the oath, as described above, and walked under the pike. They also armed themselves like lords in My Gracious Lord's upper and lower districts. They camped at Durrach and remained there several days.[7]

In 1491, the prince-abbot reported, the peasants of Kempten organized themselves in paramilitary fashion. Their actions led to an intervention by the Swabian League, a peacekeeping organization of princes, nobles, and free cities, which in the following year levied fines on the villages and thereby broke the peasants' resistance.[8]

Behind the massive resistance by the abbey's peasants lay the repressive policy of Kempten's prince-abbots, who aimed to level the socially and legally distinct ranks of freemen (*Freier*), tenants (*Freizinser*), and serfs (*Leibeigene*) into a common servile status (*Leibeigenschaft*). The prince-abbots denied the freemen and tenants their customary right to choose their own lords, as well as to marry and to move at will. The princely right to command and prohibit was here misused for political purposes, as the prince-abbots prohibited marriages between peasants of different status or from different lordships (*ungenossame Ehe*), rejected the peasants' right to move to new lands (*Freizügigkeit*), and enforced the principle of the "lesser hand," whereby children inherited the status of the legally inferior parent. Taken together, these actions meant legal disenfranchisement, and the peasants themselves cited not less than twelve hundred cases of arbitrary lowering of rank to document their legal case against the prince-abbot. The following example is characteristic of the prince-abbots' methods: "Item, Anna Reck of Westerriedt in the parish of Wittik, was a free woman on account of both her father and mother. Prince-abbot Riethain had her arrested and brought to Kempten Abbey, where he held her prisoner until she confessed that she and her siblings were servile tenants (*frey zinser*) of Kempten Abbey. Soon thereafter, when Anna Reck married Jacob Vogler, bathhouse attendant at Mengen, who is a serf of Kempten Abbey, she was then forced to become a serf, as well. Thus, Anna, a free woman, was forced first into servile tenancy and then into miserable serfdom."[9]

The conflict continued to smolder after the Swabian League's intervention in 1492. In 1523 the subjects at first refused the prince-abbot their oath, the necessary legal basis of the lord-subject relationship, and only after he promised to redress their grievances did they swear the oath and agree to obey him. Then, at the peasants' insistence in 1525, the quarrel came before an arbitrating commission, though this move foundered on the prince-abbot's refusal to deal with his subjects as a group, insisting on hearing only individual complaints. He nonetheless failed to break the peasants' solidarity, and the Kempteners streamed en masse into the great insurrection of 1525.

Since Kempten's subjects remained obdurate even after the military defeat of the 1525 Peasants' War, a new process of arbitration was begun by commissioners of the Swabian League. Its outcome was the constitution of the Kempten parliament (*Landschaft*). The commissioners recognized the subjects corporately as a contracting party, and the new parliamentary corporation's status as a legal subject was emphasized by giving it one of the two sealed copies of the Treaty of Memmingen, which embodied the arbitration's outcome. This treaty fixed the peasants' legal relationship to the abbey by regulating matters of serfdom, landlordship, rights of inheritance, the right to marry, mobility, and the level and method of taxation, which were defined largely as the peasants had demanded. The treaty was meant to abolish the conflicts that had been gathering for more than two generations around the principal themes of the agrarian constitution and taxes, and these conflicts remained the central concerns of Kempten's quasi-parliament until the early nineteenth century.

During the seventeenth and eighteenth centuries, Kempten's parliament (*Landschaft*) repeatedly had to sue to ensure that innovations introduced by the prince-abbot did not undermine the Treaty of Memmingen's stipulations. In general, the parliament successfully defended its rights. This does not mean that for three centuries years the legal forms of rural life did not change, but when change came, it was with the parliament's consent. The outcome of subject-ruler conflict in the Imperial Abbey of Kempten, therefore, was the establishment of parliamentary consent to legal changes affecting rural life—the principal subject of peasant interests—as the fundamental basis of the relationship between lord and parliament. The agreements of 1525–26 can therefore be conceived of as a constitutional law for the abbey's rural subjects.

The laws of taxation underwent even greater changes. In 1526 the shares of the prince-abbot and the parliament in imperial and Swabian League taxes were fixed at one to three, and thereafter the parliament was largely left to deal with changes in the laws concerning imperial taxes. When, following the Thirty Years' War, the parliament assumed responsibility for two groups of abbatial debts amounting to 50,000 and 60,000 florins, it became a provider of credit, for the peasants of a very small territory such as Kempten could not produce such large sums immediately. Therefore, the parliament had to resort to the money market to cover the prince-abbot's debts, paying annual interest and reducing the principal over a number of years. This role required that the parliament acquire a right to tax "of its own," assessing the sums on the members of the parliament, that is, on the peasants who were subjects of Kempten Abbey. Eventually, the parliament decided to cover its obligations to the empire and the Swabian Circle (*Kreissteuern*), which often became exorbitant in times of war, simply by borrowing on the money market. These transactions gave Kempten's parliamentary treasury a freedom of action much greater than what it originally had possessed, and by the eighteenth century, poor relief, police (troops and prison), and loans to peasants were financed largely, if not exclusively, by this institution.

The treasury and its audit procedures formed the institutional heart of Kempten's parliament. At its head stood the parliamentary treasurer (*Landschaftskassierer*), who was elected by the parliamentary "committees" (*Ausschüsse*), as they were called. The committees were made up of seven members representing the seven districts (*Ämter*) of the county, each of whom was elected by a commission from the villages and commanderies (the organizational unit for hamlets and other dispersed settlements). In Kempten, therefore, representatives were chosen exclusively through elections, which gave the Kempten parliament's policies a broad basis of support. This remained the fundamental situation, beyond all modifications and qualifications, since whenever the abbots tried to exclude peasants from the parliament or transfer its jurisdictions to the lordships, they failed. This peasant resistance was backed by the Imperial Aulic Council (*Reichshofrat*) in Vienna and by the Swabian Circle, both of which obeyed the emperor's instructions to protect the parliament's traditional rights.

Leaving aside suits before the imperial courts of law, the main forum for settling differences between ruler and parliament was the assembly for auditing accounts. Once each year the parliamentary treasurer presented his accounts both to the parliamentary commission and to the prince-abbot, the chapter, and their officials. At Kempten such audit meetings replaced the parliamentary sessions usual in the larger territorial states.

The typical features of Kempten's parliament were threefold: the social homogeneity of the parliament, which contained only peasants; the concentration on the agrarian order and taxation; and the institutional forms of the parliamentary treasury and the audit meetings. This structure helps us to understand similar parliamentary corporations in such other small German states as Badenweiler, Berchtesgaden, Hochberg, the Landvogtei of

Swabia, Rottenmünster, Ochsenhausen, Rötteln-Sausenberg, Rettenberg-Sonthofen, Rot an der Rot, Rottweil, Schussenried, Tettnang, Trauchburg, and Toggenburg—to name only those the historians have already studied.[10]

Such parliaments typically emerged in the decades between 1450 and 1525, that is, when seigneurial lordship or lordship over serfs was undergoing a simplification, as the lords strove to enrich themselves from other rights of lordship. In sum, this was the age of the formation of territorial states, even in the smaller territories. They developed naturally from governmental interventions in rural life, which is why the basic ordinance governing rural life often became the parliament's charter. This happened in the small ecclesiastical principalities of Berchtesgaden, Schussenried, Ochsenhausen, and Rot an der Rot. In just these seventy-five years, taxation, which undoubtedly helped stabilize the parliaments' positions, became a problem for these small states, which could no longer cover their obligations to the empire and to the Swabian League from existing incomes. Then, too, the old connection between imperial taxation and imperial vassalage was disintegrating. King Maximilian I (r. 1493–1519) believed that the imperial taxes, which according to traditional law had to be covered by each imperial vassal from his fief's incomes, could be transferred to their subjects.

There are obvious parallels between the forms of the common man's political enfranchisement in the small territories and those in the large ones. One central motive for parliamentary formation was the subjects' desire to fix their vital interests in the codifications of territorial law. Indeed, the formation of parliaments and the negotiation of fundamental laws for rural life were two sides of the same coin. The parliaments' second main concern was to determine the level of taxation and to distribute the tax burden by means of their own institutions. In both cases, the parliaments established their right to act in areas of state jurisdiction and interest that were vital to the early modern state, namely, finance and the legal unity of the whole territory.

The proposed comparability of function between the parliamentary institutions of small states and those of large ones has parallels in institutional structures and in the forms of representation. The parliament was based on the direct relationship between the "subjects" and the ruler and on the subjects' possession of political functions. Conceptually, the "subject" was equivalent to a (male) head of household, which meant that the prerequisite for political rights was the same in the village as in the territorial parliament. It may thus be said that the common man advanced to political representation only where he already possessed political rights in his own communal association.

Political Representation of the Common Man, 1300–1800

The political representation of the common man may be seen chronologically in two phases. First, there was a stage of institutional consolidation and of growing political significance for the estates between 1350 and the mid–seventeenth century. This was followed, in the second phase, by their gradual loss of functions and their organizational disruption between 1650 and 1800. Both movements were rooted in the territorial states' need for effectiveness, which could be achieved initially only with the parliamentary estates' help and later only through the prince's own administrative organs.

Absolutist rule, which spread through the German-speaking territories after the mid–seventeenth century, had no interest in the estates' consent to governance. In Prussia the Great Elector warned his successor, "the more you call your parliament, the more authority you will lose, because the estates always seek whatever weakens Your Highness' lordship."[11] Political practice indeed followed this advice, for Brandenburg's territorial parliament met for the last time in 1653. In most territories the parliaments were no longer called after 1700, though in some a parliamentary committee maintained a modest political existence, entirely dependent on the absolutist prince.

The parliamentary committees, which appear already in the fifteenth century to execute parliamentary decisions, gradually assumed the character of princely administrative organs from the sixteenth century onward. This happened because the parliaments no longer met or met only rarely. Originally, the committees' members held office between parliamentary sessions, and their decisions had to be confirmed by the parliament as a whole. When, however, the full parliament no longer met, the committees necessarily had to fill vacancies in their own ranks by co-optation, and their decisions had to acquire more than provisional status. When this happened, the committees could no longer be even a shadow of the old parliamentary assembly or perform its main task, the creation of consensus.

The princes moved, often methodically, against the rights of their estates because of the new self-consciousness of rulers, which was formulated theoretically in the European doctrine of the sovereignty of the state. Their desire to create a uniform body of subjects flowed from a habit of mechanically dividing human society into those who rule and those who, because of their innate inferiority, must be led, guided, and ruled. This concept of a leveled body of subjects, however, was diametrically opposed to the parliamentary idea, which reflected, and even legitimated, social, legal, and political differences.

Wherever the prince could not dispense with the estates' cooperation, he favored the nobility. Brandenburg's territorial council (*Landrat*) normally comprised only Junkers (those who held noble estates), in Austria the nobles grabbed the key positions, and in Bavaria the nobles and prelates outnumbered the burghers three to one in the parliamentary committee (*Landtagsausschuß*). Increasingly, the leaders of eighteenth-century society were exclusively nobles, and among the upper bourgeois classes there developed a pathological hunger for noble status. In eighteenth-century Austria inflationary ennoblement even became standardized under Joseph II: the title of "count" cost 20,000 florins, whereas the more modest "von" cost only 386 florins. The burghers, who had registered such great social mobility during the fifteenth and sixteenth centuries, now slipped into the social background. In tune with these developments, during the eighteenth century the communal principle declined all over the empire.

In contrast to this general trend, during the eighteenth century peasant parliamentary estates became ever more active and more effective. They were increasingly pressured, of course, by the absolutist governing practices of what were mockingly called "princelets" (*Duodezfürsten*), to which, however, they did not give way. For this successful but not readily understandable resistance there are several plausible explanations. First, the small states already possessed a uniform body of subjects, which was yet to be created

Popular Representation in Parliamentary States

in the larger states. Their social homogeneity made the smaller parliamentary estates less vulnerable than those in the large states, where the nobles and the burghers fought for decades over how to share the ever-mounting tax burden. The small states' parliaments thus proved more resistant to absolutist tendencies. A second explanation is that the de facto powers of intervention possessed by the emperor and his Aulic Council were far greater in the smaller states than in large ones. They tended to support the parliamentary estates when called upon for redress or support, because curbing the princes' absolutist tendencies helped to stabilize or even to strengthen, the imperial monarchy's influence. The empire was reduced to such means because it had lost almost all authority over the large states' rulers, who tended to follow King Frederick William I of Prussia's maxim that whoever "possessed such a formidable army as the King in Prussia did not have to obey the emperor's orders and edicts."[12]

A geographical survey of where the common man, including peasants, found political representation reveals that it existed only in the empire's western lands. The relatively great weight of the communal principle in their parliaments confirms this judgment, and it is also significant that in the east the burghers were far less important vis-à-vis the nobles than elsewhere. These observations allow us to infer that subjects achieved and maintained political representation wherever local communes had come to exercise genuinely political functions. The thesis can be confirmed in Saxony, where, despite a high level of urbanization and a very extensive princely domain, the parliaments contained no rural communes and very few cities. Characteristically, Saxon villages had not preserved their political functions, and there were even cities that failed to attain political autonomy—the chief qualification for parliamentary representation.

One final observation illustrates again the reciprocal relations of communes with political functions and parliaments based on communes. On the Baltic island of Rügen at the beginning of the fourteenth century, nobles, prelates, towns, and villages all belonged to the parliamentary estates. Later, the villages disappeared from the parliament just at the time of their reduction from political to purely economic and social units in Transelbia. This disappearance clearly expressed the logic of the system.

The principles of the German political order, which we have reconstructed, were more familiar to those who lived in early modern times than they were to the historians and political scientists of the nineteenth and twentieth centuries. At the beginning of the seventeenth century, the great political theorist Johannes Althusius (1557–1638) developed a theory of parliamentary sovereignty based precisely on these principles. In the starkest possible contrast to the more widely known and influential theory of princely sovereignty constructed by Jean Bodin (1530–1596), Althusius stood squarely in the tradition of the theory of popular sovereignty, which emerged with the political doctrines of the late sixteenth-century French monarchomachs and attained its provisional completion with Jean-Jacques Rousseau. Althusius conceived the state as a comprehensive social body (*consociatio*) that arose from the voluntary association of political units. Such units included what he called the "individual public association" (*consociatio publica particularis*), which could be identified with the rural or the urban commune. They gained standing in public law in contrast to the family, which enjoyed status only in private law, because villages and towns possessed a fourfold "sharing" (*communicatio*): of property (*communicatio rerum*), of functions (*communicatio operarum*), of law (*communicatio juris*), and of agreement (*communicatio concordiae*). For Althusius, the members of the body politic, the kingdom, the empire, or the polity were the villages, cities, and provinces, whereas sovereignty (*summa potestas*) was the executive power of the "consociated" villages, towns, and provinces. Necessarily, therefore, representation belonged not only to the nobles and the clergy but also to the burghers and the "householders' estates," that is, the peasants. By transforming the real existing character of the commune into a theoretical model of politics, Althusius had a stronger influence on the European and transatlantic development of democracy than did the ruined, hollow shell of the empire, a leftover from the era between 1300 and 1650.

Chapter 3

Popular Revolts
and Political Integration

COMMON PEOPLE were interested in helping to form territorial states because the issues of taxation and uniform legislation directly touched their way of life. But securing political rights in these areas, which meant political integration into the newly emerging state, did not always occur without violence. The Abbey of Kempten is a good example of a parliamentary state that emerged from peasant resistance, whereas the Prince-archbishopric of Salzburg is an example of a parliamentary system that was able to absorb peasant revolt without massive changes. In each case the political representation of subjects in the state presupposed a politically active body of subjects. This leads to an initial connection of parliamentary state formation with revolts. Provisionally, based on the material analyzed in chapter 2, we might formulate this connection as follows: in the empire, revolt was an answer to a defect in the parliaments' inclusiveness and to the unwillingness of princes bring to the peasants into the state.

The empire experienced many revolts, most of them by peasants and burghers. Indeed, compared with France or England, one of the empire's peculiarities was the relative infrequence of noble revolts. There were noble feuds, notably the Sickingen feud of 1523, but they were marginal in importance and were not directed against the empire. Overwhelmingly urban or rural revolts, their great number in the empire—approximately 250 urban and 130 rural revolts—far outdistanced the intensity of political resistance in other European countries.

But what were these revolts? A provisional definition must suffice until we have analyzed their essential characteristics. Revolts and rebellions—normally synonymous terms used in contrast to "revolution"—were violent actions that did not go beyond a refusal to obey, and which thus contained no desire for innovation. Chalmers Johnson, the American political scientist, calls a rebellion a spontaneous, violent act of ordinary people who reject existing conditions.[1] In his view, in contrast to a revolution a rebellion does not aim to reshape a corrupt society according to a plan or vision of a more just order. In other words, a rebellion lacks an ideology.

The revolts in the empire, needless to say, were more than simple rebellions in Johnson's sense, but, with one exception—the Peasants' War of 1525— they were not revolutions. Nor, as Winfried Schulze has pointed out, can they be adequately conceived as "irrational reactions of the peasantry," as the French historians tend to do in studies of premodern revolts in France.[2] Our approach to this subject will begin by distinguishing rural from urban revolts.

Peasant Revolts

We can identify about 130 peasant revolts in the Holy Roman Empire between 1300 and 1800, even if we count only those movements involving at least several villages. The peak era was the seven or eight decades before the Reformation, before and after which the risings were distributed fairly evenly decade by decade. Geographically, they were concentrated in southern Germany but also surfaced to a lesser extent in western and eastern Germany. The north remains in this respect unexplored territory, and the recent rash of studies on peasant insurrections has not turned up any evidence of major revolts in that region. This lack may be related to the state's policy of protecting peasants (*Bauernschutz*), by means of which since the fifteenth century some states protected viable farming operations and blocked the escalation of rents. For whatever reason, in North Germany the tensions within villages and between peasants and lord remained within limits.

Mapping the revolts chronologically and geographically reveals a remarkable pattern: revolts concentrated in the south and southwest during the later Middle Ages (1300–1525) and in the southeast and east during the early modern era (1526–1700). The regions most affected in both eras were Switzerland and Austria.

What did a typical peasant revolt look like? Peter Bierbrauer has gathered the evidence, presented it systematically, and subjected it to an interpretation. He writes that "the great mass of the revolts was characterized by a relatively long process of escalation, the identifiable phases of which represented definite stages of conflict."[3] This process of escalation can be represented by a five-stage model of revolt (fig. 6).

In stage 1 the peasants presented grievances against their ruler's exactions. If he refused to accept and redress the grievances, they might refuse to perform the oath of submission (*Huldigungsverweigerung*). Since this oath was the basis of legitimate lordship, their refusal nullified the legal basis of governance. Conflict had now reached stage 2, in which the peasants refused to pay the disputed dues or to perform the disputed labor services, because the refusal to swear the oath implied the suspension of all other obligations to the ruler. In order for the ruler to be able to govern, the matter was now submitted to arbiters or an arbitration commission, accepted by both par-

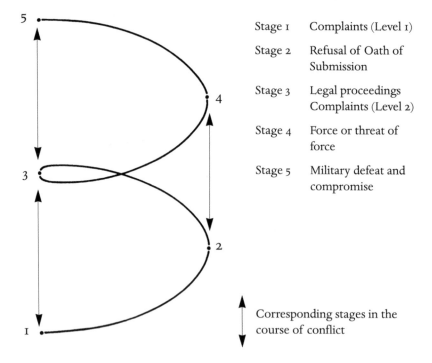

Stage 1	Complaints (Level 1)
Stage 2	Refusal of Oath of Submission
Stage 3	Legal proceedings Complaints (Level 2)
Stage 4	Force or threat of force
Stage 5	Military defeat and compromise

Corresponding stages in the course of conflict

Fig. 6. Stages of conflict in peasant revolts.

ties, and negotiations aimed to produce a settlement de facto or de jure or both. Stage 3 resembled stage 1 in that when the peasants presented and justified their grievances to the arbiters, and the ruler opposed them, the peasants had to reformulate their complaints on a more general basis. At this stage the entire relationship of subjects to lord, and not just individual complaints, came into question. If the negotiations did not produce a peaceful settlement in the form of a compromise acceptable to the peasants, the conflict moved to stage 4, the use of violence. Normally, at this stage the peasants organized themselves in military or paramilitary fashion and threatened action against the ruler. Stage 4 was analogous to stage 2 in that it posed a threat to the ruler, though now in deed rather than in word only. If the ruler's own military resources did not suffice to put down the rebels, he called upon his fellow rulers to join him in forcing the peasants to settle. This last phase, stage 5, resolved the contradictions formulated at stage 3.

The course of conflict reveals the peasants' firm will to accept risk and the remarkable courage behind rural society's efforts for the improvement of conditions. It also documents the existence of a developed political consciousness, especially in the recognition of the relative weights of the different available means. Winfried Schulze has confirmed this judgment by noting that peasants possessed "a legal consciousness oriented to the future, . . . in which the current generation accepted great burdens for the sake of future generations."[4]

It remains to be asked what interests and what goals the peasants pursued in their revolts. Although we can frame no general answer to this question at the outset, a superficial glance at the data allows us to distinguish two types of revolts: revolts against lords and revolts against taxes. This distinction is somewhat problematical because it does not comprehend all the grounds for revolts, nor does it allow for revolts of a mixed kind. Pursuing an analysis along these lines can nevertheless uncover the real core of the revolts' motivations. The first step would be to survey the peasants' grievances, the second to derive from them the subjective and objective goals of a rebellion, and the third to gain a more profound picture of the conflicts by projecting this analysis back onto the grievances themselves. This is also the method we usually employ to understand a painting, such as Botticelli's *Birth of Venus*. The picture affords a first general impression of the whole that surely comprehends something essential in it. At a second glance I notice the colors, volumes, and perspective, from which the initial impression gains new depth and precision. Even though I am not learned in art history or versed in art theory, I can now describe this painting to a friend in such a way that he or she can recognize something essential about it. Something of the same methodological character inspires our approach to the study of peasant resistance, for which the fragmentary nature of the documents may resemble the lack of art historical and theoretical knowledge in the case of a painting. Our picture of peasant revolts remains a general impression, but it is deepened by our own particular researches.

Revolts against Lords

Chronologically, revolts against lords were distributed relatively evenly across the entire era. Geographically, there was a significant shift of concentration from the west and south during the later Middle Ages to the east during the early modern era. In the late medieval southwest, the peasants most often defended themselves against their lords by means of revolts against serfdom, which was essentially the lack of liberty. Peasants complained against the lord's appropriation of all or part of a deceased peasant's estate and against restrictions on their freedom of mobility. The lords' motivation in enforcing such measures arose from the late medieval agrarian crisis, in which low grain prices meant perceptible declines in income, because the peasants' payments in kind could no longer be marketed at favorable prices. Then, too, higher real wages in the city induced peasants to flee the land in previously unheard-of numbers. High death duties and restrictions on mobility were intended to stem this flight, and they imposed a condition of unfreedom, now called "serfdom" (*Leibeigenschaft*), of a type that had not existed during the Middle Ages. This innovation fundamentally contradicted the constitutional principle of the village, which rested on the householders' free disposal of their crops and labor, which in turn rested on the right of inheritance and the right to move freely.

The early modern revolts in the regions of the East German consolidated estates (*Gutsherrschaften*) and the related Austrian form of large consolidated estates (*Großgutsherrschaften*) were touched off primarily by the imposition of higher labor dues.[5] During the eighteenth century these demands for peasant labor reached the level of six days a week in some parts of Transelbia. Jurist Johann Jacob Moser formulated the relevant division between western and eastern Germany as follows: "the common peasants or lowest class of subjects are relatively well maintained and are in the main free in some parts of the empire, such as Franconia, Swabia, the Rhine Valley, and Saxony. In other parts, however, such as Austria, Moravia, Bohemia, Lusatia, Pomerania, etc., the common rural folk live in a kind of slavery." Further, Moser wrote, "many of the latter don't live as well as the livestock of some other regions, . . . so it is hardly astonishing that such folk lose patience and organize rebellions and revolts. Indeed, what is astonishing is that they do not do so more often."[6]

If we look more closely at the revolts against seigneurial power, we see that, in what we have called stage 3 of the course of conflict, peasants presented their grievances in a more general way that challenged in principle the entire structure of governance and of agrarian life. At this point the very legal structure of rural life stood in the balance, as the example of Kempten Abbey, treated above, shows very clearly. Kempten, however, was by no means unique. In many of the South German lordships, peasant revolts were settled by means of a negotiated treaty, the character and contents of which prompt us to regard it as an agrarian fundamental law (*Agrarverfassungsvertrag*). By means of such laws the subjects collectively gained recognition as a legal person, which could form the first step toward the institutionalization of their status as subjects. At this point we can see once more the connection between rebellion and the peasants' political status. It can also be demonstrated that peasant resistance was neither an inconsequential event nor, as the older literature alleged, a step toward worsening the conditions of peasant life. The provisions of the fundamental laws, after all, could be enforced by means of appeals to the highest courts of the empire, the Aulic Council (*Reichshofrat*) and the Imperial Chamber Court (*Reichskammergericht*). And indeed, peasants often made use of these courts against their lords' excessive demands. To the degree that contractual agreements controlled conflict and limited the ruler's demands and improved the peasants'

condition—though not always as much as they wanted—we can regard peasant resistance as one agent in the regulation of agrarian life. Rebellion thus
had far-reaching consequences, even where it did not lead to the peasants'
political integration into a parliamentary state.

These agrarian fundamental laws were a phenomenon of late medieval
southern Germany. Only a few such agreements are known from eastern
Germany, mostly from the relatively well researched province of Lusatia.
The known complaints of seigneurial subjects were rarely so wide-ranging
as those from the fifteen villages of the Lusatian lordship of Sonnewalde in
1718, which directly assaulted the entire institution of the consolidated estate
(*Gutsherrschaft*) and were entirely comparable to the comprehensive cata-
logues of grievances framed by late medieval peasants in South Germany.[7]
Much more usual in the east was the requirement of an increase in labor services, so that comprehensive legal regulations comparable to the agrarian
fundamental laws in the west, were relatively rare. Indeed, comprehensive
treaties of any kind, such as the one signed between the Abbot of Neuzelle
and his subjects in 1661, were relatively rare in the east.

The more modest "successes" of the eastern peasants are explained
by the stronger position of the nobles, who in the provincial parliament
possessed a tested means of applying pressure to the territorial prince. But
the rising wave of peasant unrest in some regions—notably eighteenth-
century Lusatia, to argue again from this relatively well-documented region—did have to be dealt with eventually and did contribute something to
the princely policy of protecting the peasants (*Bauernschutzpolitik*) and eventually to the peasants' legal emancipation (*Bauernbefreiung*). In a comparative
study of these subjects across all of Europe, Jerome Blum has formulated
the hypothesis that in the dismantling of the late feudal structures of premodern Europe, peasant resistance was as important as absolutism.[8]

Revolts against Taxes

The tax revolt was the peasants' most direct response to the early modern territorial state's demands. Just as territorial state-building occurred later
than the formation of lordships, so tax revolts began later than revolts against
local lords. They apparently began with a peasant rising in Salzburg in 1462,

which was touched off by the archbishop's levy of a tax to pay for his consecration. They continued with the "Poor Conrad" in Württemberg in 1514 and the Upper Austrian peasants' war of 1596, broadening into a great wave after 1600. Even a brief survey of the individual revolts reveals a remarkable difference from the revolts against lords—their potential connection to the territorial state. The increase, both relative and absolute, of tax revolts from the end of the Middle Ages onward is easily explained by the growing degree to which the state was financed from taxes and by the steadily widening spectrum of functions that swelled the territories' permanent tax burden. Tax revolts could only occur in a developed state of the early modern type. When they occurred within a local lordship, it was either because the lordship was in the process of becoming a territorial state—a common event in the empire's western parts, as the case of Kempten Abbey illustrates—or because the lordship had in fact become a subunit of the territorial state.

A survey of the grievances yields an incomplete picture, because taxation was only one aspect of the emerging political form called "the early modern state." The existence of other important elements, such as the bureaucracy and territorial law codes, suggests that what we have called "tax revolts" formed a more complex phenomenon than can be expressed by this concept. Particularly noteworthy is the rebels' aggression against princely officials. Further, the rebels—as we see in Salzburg—hoped by refusing taxes to secure a codification of their rights and obligations on a territorial level in the form of a territorial ordinance. The term "tax revolt" thus becomes an abbreviation for disparate acts of resistance that were directed objectively against the territorial state and subjectively against taxes. The concept of "tax revolts" thus offers greater precision than the most likely alternative, "revolts against the territorial state."

If a tax revolt aimed to do more than just nullify or reduce a recent tax levy, it reached stage 3 of the conflict model, at which point peasants questioned how and by whom taxes could be levied. We know that in Salzburg, Württemberg, and Upper Austria rebels repeatedly tried to gain appropriate representation in the states' political decision-making bodies. We can infer that they aimed to secure a check on the granting and spending of taxes, which in a corporately organized state could be done only by those who were represented in the territorial parliament. This inference is supported by the absence of tax revolts in those states where peasants did possess such representation, such as Tyrol, Vorarlberg, Austrian Swabia, western Austria, and Baden. Ultimately, rebels who refused taxes wanted parliamentary representation.

These tax revolts should not be seen as mere inconsequential expressions of peasant discontent. For this the best proof is the outcome in Salzburg, where the revolts ended with the rural districts' integration into the state's parliament. Indeed, a broader view shows that what we have for brevity's sake called "tax revolts" influenced to an important degree the constitutional structures of a number of states. The Poor Conrad revolt of 1514 in Württemberg, for example, and the revolt of 1515 in Austria, led to a strengthening of parliamentary forces at the princes' expense.

Peasant Resistance

The revolt was the politically and constitutionally most effective form of peasant resistance in the Holy Roman Empire. There were, of course, also other forms of resistance, such as flight. We find flight documented from the fourteenth to the eighteenth centuries, the entire era of rural revolts. We also find other forms, such as the refusal to perform services and the illegal appropriation of dues.

A proper characterization of the peasant revolts requires two further observations. The first is that the revolts targeted whichever structure of governance was of central concern to the peasants. This could be the local lordship; it could be the larger territorial principality. In southwestern Germany the lordship was for the peasants doubtless the central political institution. By acquiring additional rights of lordship, such as mastery over serfs and low justice—often high justice, as well—the lordship was able to escape integration into a larger territorial state, to attain a position of direction subordination to the empire by becoming *reichsunmittelbar*, and to raise its lord to the rank of a territorial prince. Much the same is true for the consolidated estate of the eastern type (*Gutsherrschaft*) because, although the Junkers did not attain princely rank, their inherent prerogatives, such as judicial and executive authority, often cut the peasants off from the territorial prince, whose place the Junkers took.

Popular Revolts and Political Integration

Where seigneurial authority was weakly developed and the possibilities for the nobles and prelates to impose new obligations on their subjects and enforce them were correspondingly weak, the territorial principality and its officialdom became for the peasants the central structure of political governance. This was true in the Prince-archbishopric of Salzburg, in the Duchy of Württemberg, and partly also in Austria. It is notable that where the revolts targeted the territorial principality, they lost their exclusively peasant character. Marketplaces took part in the Salzburg revolt, and lesser burghers from the district towns (*Amtstädte*) participated in Württemberg's Poor Conrad revolt of 1514.

The second observation about the peasant revolts is that not only did they represent an attitude of defiance, they were far more a sign of fundamental contradictions between the value systems of different social classes. This is especially clear in revolts against seigneuries, which developed as struggles between peasants and lords. Both in late medieval southwestern Germany and in early modern eastern Germany, this type of revolt targeted a labor system based on servility and command from above, which was tending to reverse an earlier achievement of relative freedom and self-rule. At stake in such struggles was an organization of labor congenial to the commune, which the peasants wished either to maintain or to restore. The other form of revolt, the tax revolt, was bound up with the notion that the political order must rest on a broader consensus, to achieve which the peasants ought to be integrated into the state by means of the parliament or a similar institution.

In all cases, therefore, we find that our three chief categories—the commune, the parliament, and revolts—are connected in the closest possible way.

Urban Revolts

Urban revolts outnumbered peasant rebellions. Comparing them is only partly valid, however, because whereas an urban revolt usually affected only one city, peasant rebellions affected much larger areas, often many villages.

Across the five centuries from 1300 to 1800, urban revolts followed a uniform course. Burghers who had been excluded from the magistracies assembled, presented their grievances and demands to the city council, and elected burghers' committees. Then came negotiations with the council, which led either to constitutional changes or to a crushing of the revolt. It was utterly typical of urban revolts that the common people wanted to acquire, preserve, or win back political rights in the urban commune. In sum, therefore, one can say that the urban revolt was an attempt to vindicate the communal principle that had always obtained in the village, namely, the equality of all (male) householders.

Approximately 250 urban revolts have been identified during these centuries. Geographically, they affected northern, southern, western, and eastern Germany to similar degrees. Chronologically, the concentrations lie in the fourteenth century and the first half of the sixteenth century (fig. 7). The fourteenth-century revolts were closely connected to the guild struggles, whereas those in the sixteenth century were usually related to the Protestant Reformation. Urban rebellions also varied depending on what kind of town was involved. It is noteworthy, for instance, that nearly all of the imperial free cities experienced revolts, but only the larger territorial cities did so. [9] The smaller free cities of the order, say, of Leutkirch, which had only a few thousand inhabitants, experienced no revolts at all. One can therefore hazard the conclusion that those cities that had the most strongly developed governmental structures were especially susceptible to revolt. This applies to the free cities but not to all of the territorial cities, only the larger, economically more powerful, and therefore politically more autonomous ones. This conclusion confirms from another point of view the primarily political character of urban revolts, which is already recognizable in their typical course of development.

It is another thing entirely to analyze the urban revolts chronologically, because, unlike the peasant revolts, they betray no important changes in causes or motives. Following Erich Maschke, who studied only the period down to the mid–sixteenth century, we can sketch a model of urban revolt in four phases: the guild revolts, the revolts of "social protest," the revolts of the Reformation era, and the revolts of the seventeenth and eighteenth centuries. The arguments for distinguishing precisely these phases are not especially compelling, the less so because Maschke himself drew parallels

Popular Revolts and Political Integration

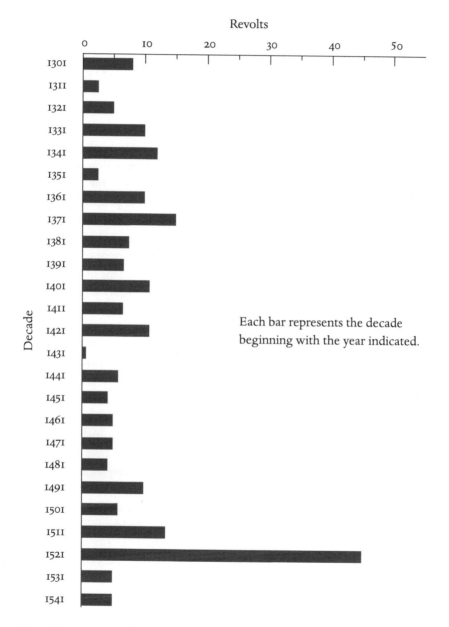

Fig. 7. Urban revolts in Germany, 1300–1540. (Translated from Erich Maschke's "Die Städte am Ausgang des Mittelalters," 40 n.206.)

between the revolts of the Reformation era and those of late Middle Ages in a way that emphasized continuities rather than differences. Revolts from quite distant eras, such as the fourteenth and the seventeenth centuries, often cannot be clearly distinguished from one another. The guild revolts of the earlier era aimed at political participation in the magistracies of the guilds for a large portion of the citizenry, whereas in the seventeenth-century revolts, such as the Cologne revolt of 1685, in the formulation of Gerhard Schilfert, "the guildsmen attempted to prevent the concentration of power in the hands of individual magistrates and to break the domination of the patricians by establishing a permanent organ of supervision by the burghers."[10]

The most important groups of urban revolts were probably the guild revolts or civic struggles of the fourteenth century and those connected with the Protestant Reformation. In the guild revolts the equality of householders was first developed as a constitutional principle, an event of fundamental importance from the standpoint of this book. By means of a successful guild revolt, a city that had been ruled by patricians—mostly seminoble families descended from ministerials[11] who had served the city's overlord—was transformed by means of the communal principle. At this point, the horizontal-communal ties began to supplant the vertical-feudal ones, so that the urban commune began to replicate the rural commune. This process was already recognized by Georg Below more than a hundred years ago.

The significance of the urban revolts of the Reformation era lay in the commune's attempt to translate the gospel into life. This urban understanding of the gospel did possess a double face, since the gospel as pure doctrine operated not only in the spiritual realm but also as a binding rule by which the earthly realm should be justly ordered. This meant that both social order and government had to be reformed in the light of the gospel. With these urban revolts, as with the others, a deeper analysis of the subject reveals a constant center to the revolts, the demand for full political enfranchisement (*Mündigkeit*) of the burghers.

Urban and rural revolts thus had a common target, the central political authority. This explains why in the territorial cities having only weak political rights there occurred not purely urban disturbances but joint urban-rural rebellions against the common territorial ruler. The Peasants' War of 1525 supplies some of the many examples of this collaboration between urban and rural folk.

Another, quite different type of urban revolt, the journeymen's revolt, also merits mention here. Disturbances among journeyman artisans went back into the fourteenth century, but they first became common in the eighteenth century. Journeymen struggled against their masters for better conditions of work and life, and everywhere the authorities, urban magistrates, and princely regimes moved energetically against them. This routinely led to the journeymen's "secession," that is, their exodus from the city. In 1726 all of Augsburg's journeyman cobblers seceded and decamped to Friedberg in Bavaria, whereupon shoe production collapsed in Augsburg. Since this was no isolated incident, it is easy to see how such actions led to supralocal and even supraregional solidarities among the journeymen. The alarmed reactions of the authorities can be read in the legislation not only of the territorial states but also of the empire. The only law on this subject issued by the Imperial Diet between 1654 and 1802 is a recess of 1731 about the guilds; this recess can be interpreted as directed against the journeymen and their associations. To discipline the journeymen it introduced the requirement of a "clean record" (*Kundschaft*), whereby a journeyman who altered his place of employment had to give evidence of his former employment. Any master could, by threatening to refuse the credentials of his journeymen, forestall every resistance and every attempt to organize. Without such a clean record the journeyman would be suspected of belonging to the dishonorable "traveling folk," hundreds of thousands of whom coursed across the eighteenth-century German territories and unsettled the lives of settled people.

The journeymen's "exodus" from the city corresponded to the peasant's "exodus" from his lord. The earliest known example of mass flight comes from the County of Hohenzollern-Hechingen in 1584, when seventy-two peasants left their village and the county for two months and refused all demands of and obligations to their ruler. This threatened the lordship's very existence, for the prince found that he could not force his subjects to fulfill their obligations. Although such peasant exoduses grew more frequent during the eighteenth century, they never became a truly common remedy for rural society, because, unlike journeymen, peasants were relatively immobile and had more to lose: their farms.

These revolts by journeymen presage a new era, the era of wage labor, strikes, and class society. The problems that began to emerge in such events were no longer those of premodern society. Indeed, the very visibility of such revolts during the eighteenth century shows that the old society based on estates or orders was being subjected to problems it could not solve.

Chapter 4

Subjects and Rulers:
A New View of German History
"From Below"

PERIODIZING HISTORY means presenting the character of an epoch, what was typical of it, by dividing it into meaningful chronological units. As long as cultural and intellectual history dominated historical studies, it was sensible to speak of "the Reformation era" or "the Age of Enlightenment." When political history was dominant, one spoke of the "Age of Religious Wars" or the "Age of Absolutism." And when the focus became the great personality as the historical actor, one wrote of the "Age of the Fuggers" or the "Age of Louis XIV." Whatever their accuracy for their own special subjects, such concepts of periodization have no connection to the majority of society. What, for example, did Enlightenment, Absolutism, or Louis XIV mean for the peasants?

Periodizing history "from below," that is, based on the material conditions of life and the peasants' and burghers' possibilities for development, requires us not to overturn traditional schemes of periodization but to supplement them. This aim is by no means as original or disruptive generally as it might seem to be in the specific context of German historiography. Indeed, when modern ethnologists and social anthropologists seek to divide world history into useful and distinguishable systems, they commonly periodize history from below. One such effort is the idea of "peasant society" postulated by Eric Wolf as a worldwide social formation posed between primitive society and industrial society. Marxist theory does the same when it constructs social formations such as feudalism, capitalism, and socialism. It must be conceded that all such schemes of periodization, which begin with the infrastructure of the whole society, are relatively unhelpful in explaining internal structures in a meaningful way. The Marxist concept of feudalism, for example, which covers a thousand years of history, is at best useful for periodization on the grandest of scales, a sort of macroperiodization. Can such schemes be supplemented by meaningful microperiodizations? We can examine this question within the geographically limited framework of the Holy Roman Empire.

On a macrohistorical scale we can doubtless characterize the period from 1300 to 1800 as a coherent unit, which we can see clearly if we inventory the leading characteristics of the previous and the succeeding ages. Before 1300 the most important social, economic, and political characteristics were collective unfreedom for the vast majority of the population, the determination of their labor by others, and their political adolescence in a nearly totally agrarian world. After 1800 the analogous characteristic was individual freedom, which affords the subject the possibility of economic and political action in an increasingly industrialized world. The epoch between 1300 and 1800, by contrast, was characterized by a relative freedom of action, self-determined forms of labor (either peasant or artisan forms of family enterprise), and the political enfranchisement of the (male) householder. The institutional framework that made this possible was the commune, and for a concept adequate to this fact we employ the term, "communalism." The epoch between 1300 and 1800, therefore, can be characterized "from below" as the age of communalism. The term cannot express, of course, a complete view of the era, but it possesses approximately the same explanatory power as the terms "feudalism," "capitalism," and "absolutism."

We can roughly distinguish three phases in the history of German communalism: 1300 to 1550, 1550 to 1650, and 1650 to 1800. The first era witnessed the development of the communal-associative model of government, the second its challenge by the German princes and their appropriation of the Protestant Reformation, and the third its rout by the absolutist state.

The Communal-Associative Model: Germany's "Third Way"

The era from the end of the thirteenth to the middle of the sixteenth century witnessed repeated, unsuccessful attempts to form the state on the basis of the communal principle and the association of communes with one another. This communal-associative model may be regarded as a third alternative after empire and territory, and emperor and territorial prince, which are often regarded as the only two options.

The Swiss Confederacy represents one of the early realizations of the communal-associative model. In 1291 the three Forest Cantons of Uri, Schwyz, and Unterwalden renewed an older league that possibly reached back to the mid–thirteenth century. The Forest Cantons were peasant communes having political functions, which through direct relationship to the empire had acquired a political freedom of action greater than what other peasant communes possessed. In 1291 the three cantons pledged mutual aid against violence from inside and outside the member cantons, common action against feuds, extortions,[1] robbery, and the appointment of foreign judges. In 1315 they stipulated that no member land would recognize a lord without the others' approval and that the members were bound to a common policy concerning external relations and league affairs. Their chief concern was to maintain peace and law within the league of the three Forest Cantons and to defend their sworn association (*Eidgenossenschaft*) from external threats.

Political functions, elsewhere assumed by the prince, were here taken over by the corporations of the three lands. The mid-fourteenth-century expansion of this league to an eight-member association through the inclusion of cities brought no essential constitutional changes, though it did ensure the confederacy's de facto permanence by adding the economic, political, and military weight of the free cities of Zurich and Bern. The combination of rural and urban communes proves, incidentally, that these different forms were in principle compatible.

Roughly contemporaneously with the Swiss Confederacy, there arose in 1283 a combination of the nearly autonomous parish communes (*universitas terrae Ditmarciae*) of Ditmarsh in East Frisia. The parishes of Ditmarsh possessed judicial and legislative authority and the power to decide peace and war, and their association gradually reduced the prince-archbishop of Bremen's superior authority to a mere formality. Nothing shows this more clearly than does Emperor Sigmund's invitation to Ditmarsh to attend an Imperial Diet in 1430. The Imperial chancellery thereby recognized Ditmarsh as directly subject to the empire, that is, possessed of a status comparable to that of the imperial estates and the imperial free cities. In 1447 the Ditmarsh association established a territorial law (*Landrecht*), created a superior court over the parish courts, and instituted parliamentary representation for external and military affairs. In contrast to the Swiss Confederacy, however, Ditmarsh could not maintain its political autonomy against the imperial princes in northwestern Germany. The land did win several victories over princely armies, but in 1550 Duke Adolf of Holstein conquered Ditmarsh and ended its status as a self-governing land. It was ruined less by internal political disintegration than by its incompatibility with the overpowering, feudally structured political environment.

Much the same is true of the federation called the League above the Lake.[2] It formed in 1405 in the Rhine Valley south of Lake Constance from an alliance of the land of Appenzell with the imperial free city of Saint Gall, after the Appenzellers had revolted against their lord, the abbot of Saint Gall. In two battles fought in 1403 and 1405, the Swabian cities and the Archduke of Austria respectively sought to force the Appenzellers back under the abbot's lordship. But the peasants won both battles and declared their independence from the abbey. The league established in 1405 spread rapidly to embrace almost all of the rural and urban communes of the region south of Lake Constance, plus the land of Vorarlberg, which lay eastward of the Rhine. The constitution of the League above the Lake, a sibling of the Swiss Confederacy, created a statelike formation in the Lake Constance region that not only operated without the feudal principle but actively opposed it all over this region. As the league spread out of its core region in Appenzell and Saint Gall toward the Arlberg and into the Allgäu and Upper Swabia, it embarked on a radical policy of razing the castles of the nobility.

The expansion of this new state posed a threat felt to be fundamental by the Swabian nobility, who gathered all of their strength against it in the Society of Saint George's Shield. This association strove to unite nobles in an area stretching from the Black Forest to the Lech River Valley against the Appenzellers. In the decisive battle near Bregenz in 1408, the nobles crushed their enemies, and the League above the Lake was destroyed.

The final, most important, and most dangerous attempt to realize the communal principle in the form of states occurred during the revolution of

1525, commonly called the German Peasants' War. All political programs developed during this insurrection advocated two principles: the commune as the basis for forming political will, and election as the criterion for distributing political offices. The communal-associative model came most clearly to the fore in the regions of small territories, mainly in Swabia, Franconia, and the Upper Rhine. The Christian Associations that arose in Upper Swabia, the Black Forest, Alsace, and Franconia advanced claims that warrant considering them to be statelike formations within the empire. Their basis lay in urban and village communes, members of which came together to form troops (*Haufen*). This military term initially designated a fighting unit, though, as the structure of feudal lordship collapsed, the troops of 1525 came to regard themselves as political associations. The troops' leaders, who were elected by the villages and towns, assumed the functions traditionally exercised by the lord, whether prelate, noble, or prince. Once formed politically, the autonomous troops came together to form the federal Christian Association in Upper Swabia, which in size was comparable to the Swiss Confederacy or the Duchy of Württemberg.

The Christian Association was the most logical and direct translation of the communal principle into political structure. In 1525 this also happened in what we are calling the constituted states, that is, those that already possessed a parliamentary constitution, such as Salzburg and Württemberg. In such states the existing institutional framework was retained, but the decision-making bodies, the parliaments, were completely or partly altered. In such cases, the urban communes and rural communes (and sometimes mining communes) usually formed the new basis of the state. They elected delegates to the parliamentary assembly, which in turn elected a parliamentary regime that governed the land, with or without the territorial prince. The principles of the communal-associative model, with communes and elections, became the definitive elements of the constitution.

The Peasants' War of 1525 was the high point of the German movements to build states on a communal basis. It was also the last. The Grey Leagues or Graubünden presents a special case but not an exception, because their formation was also completed in the context of 1525.[3] In 1526 one of its three parts, the Gotteshausbund, established itself as a republic. The bishop of

Chur and his cathedral chapter were held to be deposed from their political functions, so that what had long been a parliamentary state, in which the rural communes and the commune of the city of Chur had functioned as parliamentary estates, abolished its princely component and became a republic.

This trend toward the communal-associative state found its place in contemporary literature, political thought, and theology. Increasingly, as an awareness of the tensions created by the opposition between communalism and feudalism spread through the land, it assumed a progressively more visible place in contemporary thought.

Günther Franz (d. 1985), a leading modern historian of the Peasants' War, concluded that "perhaps in no other era did literature occupy itself so intensively with the peasant as it did during the late Middle Ages."[4] Literature acquired an ambivalent attitude, portraying the peasant as the object both of praise and of satire, though the general tendency was unambiguously toward a higher appreciation of the peasant's worth. For the mystical theologian Johannes Tauler (1300?–1361), the peasant, who "must leave the village and earn his sour bread with yet sourer labor," stood closer to God than the lazy priest. Peter Suchenwirt (d. 1395?) posed the critical, penetrating question, "What would the lord live off, if there were no peasants?" The Nuremberg mastersinger and gunsmith Hans Rosenplüt (1400?–1470?) placed at the pinnacle of creation the peasant, whom the emperor must strive to equal, and to whom God will grant the crown. On the title page of a 1508 printed work by Josef Grünpeck (1473?–1532?), secretary to Emperor Maximilian I, a peasant stands at the altar, while the priest follows the plow (plate 4). This not only symbolizes a world turned upside down, it also represents a widespread judgment on the proximity of the peasant, the common man, to God.

This praise of the peasant reached its peak in poetry. The socially critical tendency in poetry was expressed by the late medieval saying, "When Adam delved and Eve span, / Who was then a gentleman?" With many variations, this couplet became the common coin of social criticism during the fifteenth and sixteenth centuries. It not only presumed an originally egalitarian society, thus reinforcing the principle of the commune, it also described the labor of Adam and Eve as the original, godly activity of the order

Plate 4. The labors of Adam and Eve, twelfth century. Initial A ("Adam") from the beginning of the Orosius Chronicle (manuscript from Zwiefalten Abbey), folio IV, Landesbibliothek, Stuttgart. (Bildarchiv Foto Marburg, no. 246.040)

of creation. Labor and leisure, equality and inequality, were correlative concepts; labor and equality went together, as did leisure and inequality. In this context the common man stood in contrast to the ruling estates of the nobility and clergy (plate 5).

Literature, and especially poetry, wore a double social face, posed now on the feudal ruling classes' side, now on that of the common man. Both positions were theologized during the mounting confrontation with the rebellious peasantries and urban communes. The contrary peasant was compared to the rebellious Lucifer, the exploiting lord to the tyrant Nimrod.

Political thought, most of which probably deserves the more modest title of political writing, very clearly portrayed the damages wrought by the feudal order. The authors who took part in the late medieval reform debates

Das erſte Capitel von der verenderung
aller ſtende der Criſtenheyt/ die mag gewert werden auß den ſichtßarn
zaychen des hümels

Plate 5. Reform of the All the Estates of Christendom. From W. Grünbeck,
Ein Spiegel der natürlichen, himlischen und prophetischen Salbungen aller Trüb-
salen, Angst und Not, die uber alle Stende . . . in kurzen Tagen geen werden
(Nuremberg, 1508).

sought, less ambiguously than the poets, to enhance the power of the antifeudal groups of burghers and peasants. This idea was already vaguely
sketched in the anonymous tract titled the *Reformatio Sigismundi*, composed
at Basel in 1439 and published several times. It portrayed the monarchy's
weakness as a consequence of the princes' appropriation of the monarch's

rights. The reorganization of the empire, it was said, had to begin with the imperial knights, who had been part of a conception of a nobility of service, and with the imperial free cities. One cannot find in this tract any coherent, well-thought-out plan of reform, because the argument moves from subject to subject without establishing connections among them. The anonymous author nonetheless did make an advance beyond older programs for reform. He advocated a complete abolition of servitude in town and countryside, translating into law the very principle that lay at the commune's heart. In this work, as occasionally in others, the justification of equality was derived from the very order of creation. The author also rejected invasions of the village commons and their privatization by feudal lords—a serious violation of the village's communal property—as unjust acts.

In his work on the reform of the empire, called *De concordantia catholica*, Nicholas of Cusa (1401–1464) took a different starting point and attained a higher level of analysis.[5] He began with a weighty axiomatic assumption: humanity is the embodiment of law, by nature free and endowed with reason. From this it followed that legitimate lordship could be based only on free agreement and consent expressed through the electoral principle. This is why cities assumed a much higher place in his scheme for imperial reform than they did in the actual imperial constitution, in which the imperial free cities played almost no role. Cusa would have given the cities representation at all levels of the empire—in the Circles, in the Imperial Diet, and in other imperial assemblies.

In writings from the later fifteenth century, the countryside, along with the city, assumed an ever stronger role in the eyes of imperial reformers and utopian writers. In a description of the imperial constitution composed around 1450, Alsatian jurist Peter of Andlau represented the four great cities—Cologne, Regensburg, Salzburg, and Constance—as four peasants who sustained the empire. Like other writers, he derived the name of Cologne from "pillar" (*colonus*), and he merged the burghers and the peasants iconographically into a visual representation of the common man (plate 6).

Another writer, the anonymous Upper Rhenish Revolutionary, found the empire's salvation in the common man. Writing between 1498 and 1510, the author, who was probably an Alsatian, framed his charges against the clergy,

Coellen des hilligen Roemschen
Rijchs gebuyr. buman. buhere.

Plate 6. Imperial eagle with the arms of Cologne on its wings, and in the middle a peasant with scythe and flail. From *Die Cronica van der hilliger Stat van Coellen* (Cologne, Johann Koelhoff the Younger, 1499; reprinted, 1972), fol. 142.

the princes, and the nobles. Though riddled with contradictions, the text does contain a main line of argument, though not always a clear one. The empire had to be reformed by means of a revolution accomplished by the Fraternity of the Yellow Cross, which was to be composed "mainly of men from the social order of the common man."[6] In the empire as conceived by the Upper Rhenish Revolutionary, roughly speaking, only the common man and the emperor survived. Even the emperor appeared as a vague and almost mythical figure who would emerge from the Black Forest.

Shorter in temporal perspective but more concrete in conception was a 1523 tract, also anonymous, titled "The German Nation's Need."[7] Restricting himself in the main to the empire's judicial administration, the author appreciably upgraded village and other rural communes. The reformed Imperial Chamber Court of sixteen judges would be dominated by the imperial free cities, the territorial cities, and the villages in the proportion three to three to four, whereas the princes, counts, and knights together would appoint only two judges each, giving the commons a ten to six superiority over the nobles. The same principle would be extended to the entire administration of imperial justice.

At the end of this tradition, in many respects, stands the utopian work "On the New Transformation," printed at Leipzig in 1527.[8] Almost certainly composed in 1525, the year of revolution, it proposed to reform the entire world on the dual basis of the commune and the electoral principle. Whereas the author of the *Reformatio Sigismundi* had seen the imperial free cities as the sole font of imperial renewal, this author conceived the world reformed as a thoroughly peasant world. It is suggestive that nowhere else in the utopian literature of the Renaissance, neither in More nor in Rabelais, did the peasant attain such a high position. The "New Transformation" projected a future state struggling for realization but doomed never to be realized: the state founded on the peasant commune.

This project of communalizing transformation gained a powerful theological support from Martin Luther (1483–1546) and his followers—Martin Bucer (1491–1550), Huldrych Zwingli (1484–1531), and other Protestant reformers. Central to Luther's theology was his doctrine of justification, the political and social relevance of which arose from its postulation of an absolutely private act of grace and faith between God and the individual. This yielded three essential notions for communalization. First, the consequent religious equality of all Christians emphasized the principle of equality, just as the urban and rural communes did, though, of course, Luther's notion of equality had a purely transcendental intention. Second, the church was deprived of some of its essential functions, such as the mediation and administration of grace, which made the clergy as an estate superfluous and posed a considerable threat to the entire concept of a society based on estates. Third, since the old church universal was necessarily no longer the essential Christian organization, this role could be assumed by the commune.

Luther presented his idea clearly in a tract of 1523, "That a Christian Assembly or Commune Has the Right and the Power to Judge All Doctrines and to Call or Dismiss Teachers, along with Justifications from the Bible." In order to judge doctrine, Luther wrote, "or to call or depose teachers or pastors, one must not have recourse to human justice, laws, customs, usages, or traditions, etc., whether issued by pope, emperor, prince, or bishop, no matter whether half the world, or even the whole world, has obeyed such things for one year or a thousand." Luther tried to sweep away a thousand years of tradition, unavoidably leaving behind a vacuum. What could be done to fill it? Saint Paul, Luther continues, approved "no doctrine or teaching, unless it is tested by the community, to whom it is preached, and found by them to be sound." The commune or community, therefore, was to decide about true doctrine and true preachers. Since "God must not be asked to send new preachers from heaven, we must hold to the Bible and call up from among ourselves and establish such as are found to be able, and whom God has granted understanding and endowed with talents.[9] If the community could decide about the true interpretation of the gospel, should it not also decide upon the proper form and social foundations of the state?

No one ever gave the communal principle a more apt theological foundation than did Luther. His communal principle, however, was unthinkable without the previous history of the commune in Germany, and it was not and could not have been based on a theological deduction. If it had been, Luther himself could not have suspended it, as he did just a few years later.

The Rulers Disfranchise Their Subjects

As cited by Luther in a 1523 comment on Thessalonians, Saint Paul approved "no doctrine or teaching, unless it is tested by the community to whom it is preached, and is found by them to be sound." Three decades later, the imperial estates at the Diet of Augsburg in 1555 agreed to a different principle: "whose the rule, his the religion."[10] Although Luther originally envisaged a religious reformation based on free decisions by emancipated Christians, the German princes were able to pervert this vision into a new confessional and doctrinal principle for the empire. Hence, the commune did not become the community of faith, but instead, the state determined the confession, the belief, of its subjects.

How can we explain so radical a transformation of Protestant religion? The answer lies somewhere in the dialectical structure of Luther's theology and ethics, which unleashed both emancipatory and regressive forces. Two aspects of Luther's theology shaped his ideas about subjects and rulers. On the positive side was his original understanding of community, which in treating the relationship between God and humanity emphasized the categories of the equality of human beings and the community of the baptized. These principles manifested themselves in the community's decisions about true doctrine and the hiring and firing of pastors, which completed a line of thought that had been developing in the late medieval political commune. Further, Luther reevaluated labor by interpreting it as a service to one's neighbor and a fulfillment of God's order of creation. This concept was enhanced by his rejection of monastic disdain for the world in favor of a meaningful way of human life in this world. He thereby embedded a life in this world within a theological worldview that gave the laboring common man a higher value and set him above the empire's leisured classes. This was the positive side of Luther's dialectic.

On the negative side, Luther also taught the inviolability of authority and rejected the right of resistance even when one's very life was in danger. Authority was for Luther ipso facto a divine creation, a necessary principle of order in a sinful world. It protected the created world from destruction, and to obey it was to serve God. The political naïveté of Luther the theologian, who never really reflected on the best form of the state, is revealed in his transposition of the problem of controlling power into a problem of the ruler's conscience. This reflected his conservative economic and social ethics, according to which each person had to remain in his or her occupation, estate, and office and be satisfied with a secure and sufficient living.

We know that in German Lutheranism the socially and politically regressive components of Luther's thought won the day. How did this happen? The communal-associative model, which had been gaining greater profile and strength in late medieval political associations such as the Swiss Confederacy, did in fact draw, in the minds of his contemporaries, a new theological legitimacy from Luther's theology. It seemed natural, in an age so moved by religion and theology, that the approbation of a famous theologian was an authentication of the highest order. Luther thereby enormously strengthened the communal principle and accelerated its passage toward political autonomy, so much so that during the revolution of the common man in 1525, the movement disrupted the whole structure of authority.

This event jeopardized the survival of the feudal classes to a degree unprecedented in European history. But princes and lords overcame its threat by military action, thereby forestalling the formation of states on a communal-associative basis. The religious reformation, thus withdrawn from the communes, became a matter of state. Despite occasional dissent from church historians, there is general agreement that, as Günther Franz wrote, "the Peasants' War opened the way from the living communal Christianity of Luther's early days, most obviously expressed in the demand for free election of pastors, to the hierarchical rigidity of the territorial church."[11] Or, as Max Steinmetz (d. 1990), a leading East German historian, put it, "with the defeat of the early bourgeois revolution in Germany,[12] . . . the revolutionary unity of reformation and Peasants' War was dissolved. Although the revolutionary forces were crushed, the moderate-bourgeois type of the Reformation spread in the form of Lutheranism, which submitted to the strengthened power of the princes, throughout large parts of Europe."[13]

These judgments are based on facts. Under pressure of the Revolution of 1525, Luther and his closest supporters, such as Philip Melanchthon

(1497–1460) and Johannes Brenz (1499–1570), demanded the drafting of church ordinances in cooperation with the rulers and left their execution in the territorial princes' hands. A reformation based on the emancipated commune was not even mentioned; the pastors were installed from above, like other state officials; and the entire Protestant Reformation was managed by the princes. The pure gospel, love of neighbor, and obedience to authority became interchangeable concepts. The imperial estates in Alsace expressed this newly discovered identity just after the Peasants' War, when they asked that in the diocese of Strasbourg "the parishes be supplied with pious, honorable priests, who will preach only the holy gospel and the epistles purely and clearly without human additions, and give instruction in the honor of God and in obedience to temporal authority."[14]

To speak of the "state's takeover of the Reformation" is to refer to the relatively complicated, gradual process by which the Protestant Reformation was accommodated to the territorial princes' interests. The territorial state and its representatives successfully tried to emphasize the Protestant reformers' theology, but even more so their ethics, in order to make their own authority more secure. Luther became a prime force against economic progress in the form of early capitalism in the cities, against social mobility and the reduction of social differences among the estates, and against all criticism of authority. The Lutheran territorial churches belonged, therefore, to those "ecclesiastical communities which, by virtue of their type of organization, are very closely tied to the authoritarian interests of princes and noblemen upon whom they are dependent." Max Weber pointedly characterized this Protestantism as representing "very largely a reaction against the development of modern rationalism, of which the cities were regarded as the carriers"—and, we can add, against the communal principle.[15] The antagonism between the communal reformation and the reformation within the territorial states, which could not be resolved by means of a synthesis, makes it reasonable to suggest that in its finally fixed form the Protestant Reformation came to enjoy a great affinity to princely and noble lordship. This can be confirmed by looking at historical maps of the Protestant Reformation. Eastern Germany obviously received Lutheranism to a greater degree than did the west. Or, to put it another way, the region of greatest noble power became more exclusively Lutheran than the empire's western regions, where rural and urban communes played a greater role. It is also worth mentioning in this connection that the Austrian nobles in the eastern parts of the Habsburg monarchy became Protestant, whereas those in the western Austrian regions, stretching from Tyrol to Alsace, did not.

The adaptability of Lutheran ethical norms to German noble lordship can be demonstrated in another way. The refeudalization of the empire during the early modern era was primarily a Transelbian phenomenon, the form of which is inconceivable without the ideological framework of Lutheranism. Sigmund von Frauendorfer has noted that

> the authoritarian idea, which became highly developed among Luther's orthodox followers and contributed to strengthening the princes' growing power, . . . also supplied the lords and Junkers with a large measure of self-assurance. This attitude insulated them from any doubts that their position required any kind of justification vis-à-vis their subjects. The biblical norm, that all authority comes from God, was all too frequently interpreted by the Lutheran theologians as though it did not affect the rural ruling class. These classes, bolstered by their double role as estate owners and holders of judicial and police powers, could rest easy in feeling themselves to be embodiments of the "Christian ruler" (*magistratus christianus*).[16]

What for Luther had been the inseparable counterpart of this conception of authority, concern for the common good and for one's subjects, could easily evaporate if an unusually strict personal conscience did not restrain self-interest.

It is in any case noteworthy that in the regions of the East German large estate (*Gutsherrschaft*), by the mid–sixteenth century there began the systematic dispossession of free peasants (*Bauernlegen*) by the nobles. Whereas in earlier times only vacant peasant holdings had been incorporated into the noble estates, now the peasants were more or less systematically bought out and expelled, to a degree that prompted Wilhelm Abel to speak of a "second wave of German peasant settlement" by the refugees in the regions between East Prussia and Silesia.[17]

The dispossession of these free peasants naturally deprived noble estates of the labor necessary to work the lands appropriated by the nobles. This led to raising the labor dues on the remaining peasants and, necessarily, to limiting the mobility of both the peasants and their children. The labor dues of the peasants and services of their children made possible the transformation of the noble estate, with the concomitant growth of hereditary servitude and forced labor. The decisive period for this development was not, as has frequently been alleged, the seventeenth and eighteenth centuries, but the second half of the sixteenth century. Coincident with the Protestant Reformation two institutions appeared in the East German agrarian system: the obligation to plow (*Schollenpflichtigkeit*) and forced labor (*Gesindezwangsdienst*). "Viewed purely pragmatically," Abel has written, these practices "opened a way to reducing the incomes of the peasants and their heirs to the physically necessary minimum." That they were sometimes used for just this purpose is revealed by glances at Mecklenburg, Nearer (western) Pomerania, and Holstein, where developed a form of hereditary servitude that differed from ancient slavery only in name. Such developments naturally evoked criticism from contemporaries. Christian Friedrich Daniel Schubart (1739–1791), for example, charged the nobles with daring "to tread on the rights of man. Such things are thought and spoken of only by oriental despots, which the earth has been spewing forth since Nimrod's time."[18]

The Authoritarian State in Theory and Practice: The Road to Inferiority

The era that ended with the Thirty Years' War in 1648 witnessed efforts by the princes and nobles to maintain their confessional positions both internally and externally, as the tensions between feudal and communal principles continued in many parts of the empire. In South Germany and Austria, however, the previous peasant revolts were matched in frequency or in severity after the Thirty Years' War, as the center of gravity shifted in favor of feudalism eastward to Transelbia, Bohemia, and Austria.

The time after the Thirty Years' War witnessed two tendencies that increased the social distance between nobles and subjects and gave the notion of "subject" that pejorative flavor it would retain into the nineteenth century: first, the construction of an ideology of noble rule in what is called the "housefather" literature (*Hausväterliteratur*), and, second, the German reception of foreign court culture.

Housefather literature was a literary genre devoted to showing how a (noble) household was to be managed properly by a "housefather." Written between 1670 and 1750, it concentrated on the economic, social, and political order of the household, and economic unit that basically produced what it consumed. It was an organic whole encompassing all forms of land exploitation, including that of the forest, the waters, and the hunt. The household was also a social unit, the core of which was the family, but it also included servants, and, ultimately, the entire body of subjects could be reckoned as part of it. Finally, the household was a political unit insofar as the householder, the pater familias, "ruled" this socioeconomic unit.

Many able scholars have studied housefather literature and especially the related concept of "the whole house," in which certain of these scholars have seen the fundamental element of all Western society. Lines of continuity, to be sure, could be drawn from humanism and the Renaissance back to Hesiod, Xenophon, and Aristotle, but the ideal housefather proper also bore an astonishing similarity to the central figure of Luther's social ethics, the family father. For Luther, the figure of the family father expressed the primordial order of power in this world, to which all other orders of power could be related. The prince was thus but the housefather of a huge household, and the housefather possessed unlimited authority over his wife, children, and servants. The household, a unit of both production and consumption, operated according to the principles of moderation and sufficiency. For Luther it was ideally the peasant household.

That housefather literature owed its astonishingly wide resonance in the empire more to its connection with the Protestant Reformation than to any affinity with antiquity is suggested by the fact that nearly all of it was composed in the Lutheran areas of Germany. Many of the authors were Protestant pastors, and the others were noble owners of estates. These facts help to explain why housefather literature was composed and consumed chiefly in the region of the great estates (*Gutsherrschaften*) and the very sim-

Plate 7. Family of an estate owner at the hay harvest. From Franciscus Philippus
Florinus, *Oeconomus Prudens Et Legalis oder Allgemeiner Klug- und Rechts-verständiger
Haus-Vatter*, (Nuremberg, 1702), 1:637.

ilar large lordships (*Großgrundherrschaften*) of Austria. The geographical coincidence of the housefather literature and this kind of noble rule demonstrates their interdependence (plate 7). The identification of the housefather
with the estate owner or seigneur necessarily made all of their subjects into
minor dependents.

Ravaged by the Thirty Years' War, the Germans lost much of their self-
consciousness as a people (plate 8). After the Peace of Westphalia in 1648, the
Holy Roman Empire ceased to be Europe's center, and the dynamic impulses
of European history moved to France and England on the western edge of
Europe. Now Germany began to receive uncritically, if not slavishly, a foreign (mainly French) culture. The German reception of a Baroque noble and
court culture proved decisive for the relationship of subject and ruler, be-

cause it intensified architectonically and iconographically the principles of monarchy and aristocracy. In a sense, Bodin at last won out over Althusius in Germany. There also existed a descending gradient of cultural sophistication from the courts of such large states as Brandenburg-Prussia and Austria through the middle-sized states to the small states of western Germany, many of which—such as the petty principality of Nassau-Saarbrücken—adopted Baroque culture only during the first half of the eighteenth century. At the same time, the subjects were being driven out of the political life of the territorial state.

Plate 8. *A New Complaint of Peasants' against the Soldier's Depradations.* (Copper engraving, 1642, Germanisches Nationalmuseum, Nuremberg, Graphics Collection, no. HB 16439, box 1294)

Conclusion:
Obedient Germans? A Rebuttal

HISTORICALLY, subjects in Germany were not just faceless peasants, pawns without strategic worth whom the lords pushed about on the chessboard. On the contrary, the subjects were actors, black playing against white. This truth was recognized by everyone in the old society of estates from the emperor down to the knight. Ever since lords and subjects existed, in times of conflict the feudal lords repeatedly expressed the fear that "it will eventually come to pass that the subjects will become rulers, and the lord will have to do what they command and ordain." This comment from a seventeenth-century prior of an Upper Bavarian monastery could be replicated in other texts from the fourteenth to the eighteenth centuries. The prior warned that if things were reorganized "as his subjects wanted, they would become lords, and I would have to be their servant."[1] Behind such statements lay not only the calculated wish to portray the "underlings" as outlaws, but also the fear of being unable to withstand the challenge posed by the subjects' alternative [and conflicting] concept of a political order.

Obedient Germans?—A Rebuttal. This title contains a plea for a new, broader interpretation of German history. To regard the subjects as a relevant factor in history would be an innovation, at least in Germany. Jerome Blum has held that resistance by subjects was responsible for the dissolution of the feudal order in the empire during the eighteenth century. Barrington Moore, who takes a viewpoint that is universal, though limited to rural society, has written that "no longer is it possible to take seriously the view that the peasant is an 'object of history,' a form of social life over which historical changes pass but which contributes nothing to the impetus of these changes."[2] Moore supports his thesis with material drawn from the histories of countries on three continents. In Germany, on the other hand, historians have recently been warning us against presenting "a one-sided emphasis on the subjects" and against "the danger that now, by simply reversing the sign, history will be subjected to a heroization comparable to what the ruling groups of former centuries enjoyed."[3] These warnings against overemphasis are groundless, especially at the present time, when the Hohenstaufen and Wittelsbach dynasties are being refurbished as adornments to the nation's historical consciousness. So long as the state governments spend millions to subsidize historical exhibitions dedicated to the old ruling dynasties, while an exhibit on the Peasants' War is merely a routine matter for professional archivists, there is no danger that the wrong sort of people—the subjects—will become heroically overrepresented.[4] It is the same in scholarly historical research. Medieval history has only just discovered the study of subjects, and early modern history is very cautiously sailing in its wake. Those who study subjects do so in terms of the "lower classes," a topos that usually deals with social differences and social mobility, but hardly ever touches on these classes' political significance. Political history, by contrast, is explained by invoking the so-called primacy of foreign policy, great ideas, and major personalities. Between subjects and their rulers, it is always the rulers who enjoy the sympathy, even if sometimes the critical sympathy, of the historian.

Obedient Germans?—A Rebuttal. This statement proposes the idea of a dialectical process of subject and ruler in German history, which needs to be addressed both in national and territorial historical frameworks.

On the national level we can distinguish two phases. Seen from the subjects' point of view, an upward phase of political emancipation between 1300 and 1550 was followed by a second phase of political disfranchisement between 1550 and 1800. The latter can be understood as a reaction to the former. To the degree that subjects were organized into communes, which contained the germ of a republican form of state, their communal organization formed a latent opposition to every ruler who based his legitimacy on the feudal social order. Communalism and feudalism were not only contrary structural principles—one horizontal, the other vertical—they expressed different ideas of human nature. These ideas emerged with special clarity in their respective notions of the division of labor. Feudalism "held" the subjects in a "servile" position, as the noble lord's needs set limits to the subject's power to manage his own economy and enjoy the fruits of his own labor. Communalism, on the contrary, set the subject free in a way that allowed him to manage his own labor power and the fruits of his labor (after deducting taxes or other dues for financing a functionally adequate state). The opposition between these two notions is demonstrated by the following contrast: in western Germany economic burdens remained constant during the post-Reformation era, and the division of labor maintained its communal framework; in the east the burdens climbed steadily, and the labor system was feudalized. Labor, of course, constitutes the very condition of human existence. The very derivation of the German *Arbeit*, from the Latin *arvum*, which means a plowed field, betrays a close connection to the peasant and to the human domination of nature. Christianity looked at labor in two ways: as a completion of God's work and as a compensation for sin and means for the purification of humanity. Karl Marx viewed labor as "the life that produces life." Different conceptions of the division of labor thus expressed different forms of humanity and of culture.

The contradictions between these two ways of managing human labor and their corresponding political orders became dangerous to the entire system during the fifteenth and early sixteenth centuries, when an antifeudal communal culture arose from communalism. Its traces are found in literature, political (including utopian) thought, and theology. The attempt to translate communalism as a comprehensive social principle into a form of political constitution prompted a reaction from the feudal forces, the victory of which over the communal principle prompted and expressed itself in a new ideology of feudalism. The changes of the later eighteenth century stemmed on the whole from foreign influence and certainly reflected French influence more than it did German national tradition.

Conclusion

On a smaller scale, the same thing happened at the territorial level. Here the relationship of ruler to subjects was determined by the strength or weakness of the nobles and of the communes. The constellation of forces varied widely by time and place, which explains the great variety of forms that developed within the empire. The gross division between the west and the east was nonetheless obvious and was clearly revealed in the peasant emancipation at the beginning of the nineteenth century. At that time, the Prussian reformers' goals were to free the peasants from personal and economic dependence on the noble landowners, to close the gulf between town and countryside, and to abolish patrimonial justice. In southern and western Germany, because of the peasants' much lower degree of economic dependence on their lords and the freer condition of the crafts and trades, most places had already achieved the goals of the Prussian reforms. It was easier in the west than in the east to adapt to the consequences of the French Revolution and thereby to other western European developments. Of course, this has to be seen in political terms as well. The feudal order, as it existed in Germany between 1300 and 1800, was a less controlled form of governance than was the communal order. The commune itself represented the principle of controlled power, and where it maintained its rule, limits were set to the instrumentalization of power. "Power is in itself evil," Jakob Burckhardt (1818–1897) wrote and added the complementary thought that only outside the power state is there "true liberty."[5] A study of the history of German subjects does not suggest that his judgment is obsolete.

The German as subject—a contradiction? The contradiction is resolved by our finding that German subjects were not subjects in the modern sense of the term. The negative connotation borne by this term since the Enlightenment arose from the critical conflict with the authoritarian state based on power. The authoritarian state's expansion and aggression produces impotence and anxiety as well as servility and avoidance of responsibility, which are relatively recent phenomena in German history. In Württemberg, where absolutism arose very late, around 1800, and where the communal principle survived via the parliamentary role of the districts (*Ämter*) and main-

Obedient Germans: A Rebuttal

tained a relative balance with the territorial principality, "the subject" actually remained a positive expression. In 1818 Justinus Kerner (1786–1862) praised Württemberg as distinguished from all other German lands:

> Eberhard, the bearded one,
> Württemberg's beloved prince,
> Spoke: "My land has little cities
> And no mountains full of silver;
>
> But it hides one great treasure:
> That in the forest, yet so large,
> I can lay my head without fear
> In any subject's lap."[6]

The history of Germany during the later Middle Ages and the early modern era cannot be correctly understood, as long as the common man, the subject, is not seen as that history's principal subject.[7]

Notes

Introduction

1. *Meyers Enzyklopädisches Lexikon* (Mannheim, 1979), 24:106.

2. Kurt Tucholsky, *Zwischen gestern und morgen. Eine Auswahl aus seinen Schriften und Gedichten*, edited by Mary Gerold-Tucholsky (Hamburg, 1952), 115.

3. Quoted by F. Winterhagen, *Bauernkriegsforschung* (Darmstadt, 1981), 15.

4. Max Weber, *Economy and Society: An Outline of Interpretive Sociology*, edited by Guenther Roth and Claus Wittich, 2 vols. (Berkeley, 1978), 2:1108.

5. *Tr. note:* The author here draws on the distinction between premodern society, which was ordered into a hierarchy of legally defined status groups or estates, and modern society, which, though formally characterized by legal equality, is structured by classes derived from its economic organization. The former is called in German *die altständische Gesellschaft* or *die ständische Gesellschaft* (from *Stand* [pl. *Stände*], estate), in French *la société des ordres*.

6. *Grosses vollständiges Universal-Lexikon aller Wissenschaften und Künste*, 49 (1746), col. 2253–92.

7. E. A. Koch, ed., *Neuere und vollständigere Sammlung der Reichs-Abschiede, welche von den Zeiten Kayser Konrads des II. bis jetzo auf den Teutschen Reichs-Tägen abgefasset worden*, 4 parts in 2 vols. (Frankfurt, 1747), 1:230. The recess of a parliamentary assembly or diet was the document drafted at the end of a session. It authenticated and announced the assembly's decisions.

8. Ibid., 2:273f.

9. Horst Kohl, ed., *Die politischen Reden des Fürsten Bismarck*, 14 vols. (Stuttgart, 1892–1905), 5:234. The "recent upheaval" refers to the Peasants' War.

10. Alfred Kirchhoff, ed., *Die ältesten Weisthümer der Stadt Erfurt über ihre Stellung zum Erzstift Mainz* (Halle, 1870), 13.

11. Koch, ed., *Reichs-Abschiede*, 1:78, 155.

12. For these citations, see Peter Blickle, *The Revolution of 1525: The German Peasants' War from a New Point of View*, translated by Thomas A. Brady Jr. and H. C. Erik Midelfort (Baltimore, 1981), 122–24.

13. G. Winter, ed., *Niederösterreichische Weistümer*, part 1, Österreichische Weistümer, vol. 7 (Vienna, 1886), 78.

14. Jürgen Karbach, *Die Bauernwirtschaften des Fürstentums Nassau-Saarbrücken im 18. Jahrhundert* (Saarbrücken, 1977), 130.

15. Johann Jacob Moser, *Von der Teutschen Unterthanen Rechten und Pflichten*, vol. 17 of *Neues teutsches Staatsrecht* (Frankfurt, 1774; reprinted 1967), 1–2.

16. *Tr. note:* The "later Middle Ages" refers to the fourteenth and fifteenth centuries.

17. Moser, *Von der Teutschen Unterthanen Rechten und Pflichten*, 1–2.

18. *Tr. note:* This form of state is called a *Ständestaat* in German, that is, "a state based on orders."

1. The Commune as a Political Association

1. *Tr. note:* The author here distinguishes between the village as a residential grouping and the commune as its institution of self-governance composed of elected (male) householders. His analysis depends on a recognition that the village became the dominant rural social (and eventually political) unit only with the dissolution of the manors and the older forms of dependence.

2. *Tr. note:* The author is speaking of an ethnolinguistic region that stretches from Alsace and German-speaking Lorraine eastward to the borders of Bavaria and the boundary between the Austrian provinces of Vorarlberg and Tyrol, and from a line Stuttgart-Ulm southward to the High Alps and in a few places (the Swiss cantons of Valais and Graubünden) yet further southward.

3. Rogier Sablonier, "Das Dorf im Übergang vom Hoch- zum Spätmittelalter. Untersuchungen zum Wandel ländlicher Gemeinschaftsformen im ostschweizerischen Raum," in *Institutionen, Kultur und Gesellschaft im Mittelalter. Festschrift für Josef Fleckenstein*, edited by Lutz Fenske, Werner Rösener, and Thomas Zotz (Sigmaringen, 1984), 727–45.

4. *Tr. note:* Called in German the *Villikationssystem* after the *villicus* who administered a part of it; also called the *Fronhofsystem* after the labor services (*Fronen*) owed by the peasants.

5. *Tr. note:* Medieval Germanic law was "found" or "spoken," not "made," because it was thought to be unchanging and unchangeable. As Blickle and others have

shown, this conservative vision of law nonetheless permitted in practice a great deal of creation of new law or legislation.

6. *Tr. note:* The author here alludes to the deeply engrained tradition of regarding medieval institutions of governance as springing from an interplay of two distinct forces: the principle of lordship (*Herrschaft*), which is hierarchical and implies a vertical relationship, and the principle of association (*Genossenschaft*), which is egalitarian and implies a horizontal relationship.

7. Also called *Flurhai, Eschhai, Flurer, Schütz,* or *Flurschütz.*

8. Also called *Bauermeister, Zender, Heimbürge, Schüttemeester, Pohbuchter.*

9. Karl Siegfried Bader, *Studien zur Rechtsgeschichte des mittelalterlichen Dorfes,* 3 vols. (Vienna, 1957–73), 3:2.

10. *Tr. note:* This does not apply, as the author notes, to the "imperial villages" (*Reichsdörfer*), some groups of villages, mostly in southwestern Germany, whose inhabitants were free in the sense that they had no lord other than the emperor.

11. Michael Mitterauer, "Pfarrei und ländliche Gemeinde in den österreichischen Ländern," in *Grundtypen alteuropäischer Sozialformen. Haus und Gemeinde in vorindustriellen Gesellschaften,* ed. Michael Mitterauer, Kultur und Gesellschaft. Neue historische Forschungen, vol. 5 (Stuttgart-Bad Canstatt, 1979), 139–42. Mitterauer actually writes "Josephine pastor," referring to the reign of the Emperor Joseph II (r. 1765–90).

12. *Tr. note:* "Transelbia" encompasses the German-speaking lands east of the Elbe River, including Saxony, Brandenburg, Mecklenburg, Pomerania, Lusatia, Siliesia, and East Prussia.

13. The ruling margrave of Brandenburg was one of the empire's seven electors.

14. Herbert Helbig, *Gesellschaft und Wirtschaft der Mark Brandenburg im Mittelalter,* Veröffentlichungen der Historischen Kommission zu Berlin, vol. 41 (Berlin, 1973), 41–42.

15. Karlheinz Blaschke, "Grundzüge und Probleme einer sächsischen Agrarverfassungsgeschichte," *Zeitschrift der Savigny-Stiftung für Rechtsgeschichte, germanistische Abteilung* 82 (1965): 272.

16. *Tr. note:* The overlapping regnal dates are to be explained by the fact that Maria Theresia and her son ruled jointly over the Austrian lands and the Hungarian kingdom from 1765, the year in which Joseph succeeded his father, Francis I, as Holy Roman emperor.

17. N. M. Scherer, "Die Landgemeindeverwaltung im Fürstentum Nassau-Saarbrücken 1735–1793," unpublished dissertation, Saarbrücken (1971), 166.

18. *Tr. note:* Quoted without source.

19. *Tr. note:* The author here refers to a fixed concept of German agrarian history,

the distinction between the seigniorial holding of western and southern Germany (*Grundherrschaft*), in which the lord retained no direct rights of cultivation and drew only rents from the tenants, and the consolidated large estate (*Gutsherrschaft*) of the eastern lands, whose lord combined judicial, military, and ecclesiastical authority with lordship over unfree farmers.

20. *Tr. note:* Quoted without source.

21. *Tr. note:* The principal administrative and judicial subdivision of a German territorial state was most commonly designated by the word *Amt* (literally, "office"), of which the nearest equivalent in a state of the modern Federal Republic of Germany is a Kreis (literally, "circle"). Its chief official was the *Amtmann*.

22. Bader, *Studien*, 1:230–38.

23. On the source of this adage, see Hans Planitz, *Die deutsche Stadt im Mittelalter. Von der Römerzeit bis zu den Zunftkämpfen* (Graz, 1954), 229.

24. Franz Steinbach, "Stadtgemeinde und Landgemeinde," *Rheinische Vierteljahrsblätter* 13 (1948): 30–32.

25. *Tr. note:* The German term *reichsunmittelbar* is often translated as "immediate to the empire." In English, however, "mediated" and "unmediated" have lost much of the connotation of "indirect" and "direct," which the German words convey.

2. Popular Representation in Parliamentary States

1. Werner Näf, "Der geschichtliche Aufbau des modernen Staates," in Werner Näf, *Staat und Staatsgedanke. Vorträge zur neueren Geschichte* (Bern, 1935), 37.

2. Michael Mitterauer, "Grundlagen politischer Berechtigung im mittelaltelrichen Ständewesen," in *Der moderne Parlamentarismus und seine Grundlagen in der ständischen Repräsentation*, edited by Karl Bosl and K. Möckl (Berlin, 1977), 40–41.

3. Antonio Marongiu, "Il principio della democrazia e del consenso (Quod omnes tangit, ab omnibus approbari debet) nel XIV secolo," *Studia Gratiana* 8 (1962): 555–75; see a German translation in H. Rausch, ed., *Die geschichtlichen Grundlagen der modernen Volksvertretung*, 2 vols. (Darmstadt, 1974–80), 1:183–211.

4. Weber, *Economy and Society*, 306.

5. *Tr. note:* "Constituted" means a state possessing a parliamentary structure into which the peasants were able to insert themselves as an estate; "nonconstituted" means a state lacking a parliamentary structure until the peasants forced their own recognition as a territorial estate. The former tended to be characteristic of large territorial states, the latter of small ones. The distinction is of great analytic importance to

Blickle's study of the programs and outcomes of the Peasants' War of 1525. See Blickle, *Revolution of 1525*, chapters. 8 and 11.

6. Quoted in Peter Blickle, *Landschaften im Alten Reich. Die staatliche Funktion des gemeinen mannes in Oberdeutschland* (Munich, 1973), 171. The Val Sugana lies in Venezia Tridentina.

7. Ibid., 322.

8. *Tr. note:* "Levied fines" here translates "brandschatzte," the practice of extorting a fine in return for not burning the village.

9. Peter Blickle, "Der Kemptener Leibeigenschaftsrodel," *Zeitschrift für bayerische Landesgeschichte* 42 (1979): 601.

10. *Tr. note:* In fact, it was Peter Blickle himself who produced the definitive modern study of parliamentary estates in most of the small and tiny states he names. See his *Landschaften im Alten Reich* (chapter 2, n. 3).

11. Peter Baumgart, "Zur Geschichte der kurmärkischen Stände im 17. und 18. Jahrhundert," in Dietrich Gerhard, ed., *Ständische Vertretungen in Europa im 17. und 18. Jahrhundert*, Veröffentlichungen des Max-Planck-Instituts für Geschichte, vol. 27 (Göttingen, 1969), 143.

12. Georg Küntzel and Martin Haß, eds., *Die politischen Testamente der Hohenzollern*, 2d ed. (Leipzig, 1919), 63.

3. Popular Revolts and Political Integration

1. Chalmers Johnson, *Autopsy on People's War* (Berkeley, 1973), 8.

2. Winfried Schulze, *Bäuerlicher Widerstand und feudale Herrschaft in der frühen Neuzeit*, Neuzeit im Aufbau, vol. 6 (Stuttgart, 1980), 89.

3. Peter Bierbrauer, "Bäuerliche Revolten im Alten Reich. Ein Forschungsbericht," in Peter Blickle, ed., *Aufruhr und Empörung? Studien zum bäuerlichen Widerstand im Alten Reich* (Munich, 1980), 44.

4. Schulze, *Bäuerlicher Widerstand*, 120.

5. *Tr. note:* The term *Gutsherrschaft* is employed by German agrarian historians for the large, consolidated estates that developed in the lands east of the Elbe following the late medieval depression. There were characterized by bound labor and the unification of lordship—political, legal, economic, and ecclesiastical—in the hands of the noble lord (*Gutsherr*). Such formations were common in northeastern Germany, Bohemia and Moravia, Hungary, and the eastern (but not the western) Austrian lands. The term is normally constrasted with the "landlordship" (*Grundherrschaft*) of the empire's western

Notes

regions, in which the political rights and functions of the seignior were detached from rights over the land and concentrated in the hands of the territorial princes.

6. Moser, *Unterthanen*, 477, 496, 505.

7. Rudolf Lehmann, ed., *Quellen zur Lage der Privatbauern in der Niederlausitz im Zeitalter des Absolutismus* (Berlin, 1957), no. 14.

8. Jerome Blum, *The End of the Old Order in Rural Europe* (Princeton, 1978), 332–53.

9. *Tr. note:* This rests on the distinction between the imperial free cities (*Reichsstädte*), which lay directly under the emperor's authority and were concentrated in Swabia, the Rhine Valley, Franconia, and the northern coasts, and the territorial cities, which were ruled by territorial princes. The distinction had little to do with size, for although the empire's largest cities—Cologne, Augsburg, and Nuremberg—were free, there were many territorial cities, such as Leipzig and Görlitz, that rivaled all but the largest free cities in size.

10. Gerhard Schilfert, *Deutschland von 1648 bis 1789 (vom Westfälischen Frieden bis zum Ausbruch der Französischen Revolution)*, 3d ed. (Berlin, 1975), 32.

11. *Tr. note:* Ministerials were families of servitors of the great aristocrats and prelates of the High Middle Ages. Some were of servile origin, and many became members of the lesser nobility in the late Middle Ages.

4. Subjects and Rulers

1. *Brandschatzung*, see chapter 2, n.8.

2. *Tr. note:* In Central Europe the terms "upper" and "lower" in topographical names always refer to how the rivers flow, meaning "upstream" or "downstream." "Above the Lake," therefore, means south—toward the Alps—from the lake, which is Lake Constance.

3. *Tr. note:* The independent Rhaetian Free State was an alpine republic formed of three separate federations, one of which, the Grey League (Graubünden in German; Grigioni in Italian; Grischun in Romantsh), gave its name to the whole alliance. The other two were the League of God's House (Gotteshausbund) and the League of Ten Districts (Zehngerichtebund). It was associated with but not a member of the old Swiss Confederacy, and with the reconstitution of Switzerland after Napoleonic times it became the southeasternmost (and largest) canton. See Randolph C. Head, *Early Democracy in the Grisons: Social Order and Political Language in a Swiss Mountain Canton, 1470-1620* (Cambridge, 1995).

4. Günther Franz, *Geschichte des deutschen Bauernstandes vom frühen Mittelalter bis zum 19. Jahrhundert*, 2d ed., Deutsche Agrargeschichte, vol. 4 (Stuttgart, 1976), 125.

5. *Tr. note:* Nicholas of Cusa (1401–64), a native of Kues in the Mosel Valley, rose to become bishop of Brixen and, eventually, cardinal.

6. Gerhard Zschäbitz and Annelore Franke, eds., *Das Buch der hundert Kapitel und der vierzig Statuten des sogenannten Oberrheinschen Revolutionärs*, Leipziger Übersetzungen und Abhandlungen zum Mittelalter, series A, vol. 4 (Leipzig, 1967), 156.

7. Adolf Laube and H. W. Seiffert, eds., *Flugschriften der Bauernkriegszeit* (Berlin, 1975), 73–79.

8. Ibid., 547–57.

9. Martin Luther, *D. Martin Luthers Werke, Kritische Ausgabe* (Weimar, 1900), 11:408–11.

10. This phrase was later translated into Latin, "cuius regio, eius religio," by Joachim Stephan, a Giessen law professor.

11. Günther Franz, *Der deutsche Bauernkrieg*, 10th ed. (Darmstadt, 1975), 298.

12. *Tr. note:* The concept of the "early bourgeois revolution" was originally advanced by Friedrich Engels and reformulated by Max Steinmetz. It denotes all the movements for change in the empire between 1476 and 1535, including the early Protestant Reformation, insofar as they appear to have objectively promoted capitalism and progress toward the formation of a German national state.

13. Max Steinmetz, "Zum historischen Standort des deutschen Bauernkrieges in der Geschichte der Bauernbewegungen beim Übergang vom Feudalismus zum Kapitalismus," in *Der Bauer im Klassenkampf*, edited by Gerhard Heitz et al. (Berlin, 1975), 43.

14. Walter Gunzert, "Zwei Hagenauer Abschiede von 1525," *Elsaß-Lothringisches Jahrbuch* 17 (1938): 169.

15. Weber, *Economy and Society*, 471.

16. Sigmund von Frauendorfer, *Ideengeschichte der Agrarwirtschaft und Agrarpolitik im deutschen Sprachgebiet*, vol. 1: *Von den Anfängen bis zum Ersten Weltkrieg*, 2d ed. (Minden, 1963), 110.

17. Wilhelm Abel, *Die drei Epochen der deutschen Agrargeschichte*, 2d ed., Schriftenreihe für ländliche Sozialfragen, no. 37 (Hanover, 1964), 63.

18. Quoted without source.

Conclusion

1. Renate Blickle, "'Spenn und Irrung' im 'Eigen Rottenbuch,'" in Peter Blickle, *Aufruhr und Empörung?*, 99.

2. Barrington Moore Jr., *Social Origins of Dictatorship and Democracy: Lord and Peasant in the Making of the Modern World* (Boston, 1967), 453.

Notes

3. Volker Press, "Die Landschaft aller Grafen von Solms," *Hessisches Jahrbuch für Landesgeschichte* 22 (1977): 38.

4. *Tr. note:* The author alludes here to a series of sumptuous historical exhibitions staged with official backing in West Germany, Austria, and East Germany during the early 1980s to mark anniversaries of the Wittelsbach, Hohenstaufen, Habsburg, and Hohenzollern dynasties.

5. Jakob Burckhardt, *Weltgeschichtliche Betrachtungen,* Gesammelte Werke, vol. 4 (Basel, 1957), 29, 70.

6. Justinus Kerner, "Der reichste Fürsten," in his *Werke. Auswahl in sechs Teilen,* edited by R. Pissin (n.d.), part 2, 51.

7. *Tr. note:* In German the last phrase is more transparent than in English: "solange man den Untertanen, den Gemeinen Mann, nicht als Subjekt der Geschichte würdigt." "Untertan" means "subject" in the sense of "person placed under the authority of a ruler," and "Subjekt" means "subject" in the sense of "topic."

Glossary

Allmende—in a village, the commons consisting of woodlands and pasture

Ammann—see *Schultheiß*

Banngewalt—the general authority to command

Banntaiding—a district assembly (Austria)

Bannwart—district warden, a village policeman

Bauernlegen—the dispossession of free peasants by their lords

bebaute Flur—the cultivated portion of a village's lands

Büttel—a messenger, employed by a village commune

Dienste—the labor services owed by unfree peasants to the their lord; also *Fronen*, *Robot* (Austria)

Dorf—a village

Dorfgemeinde—a village commune, commonly governed by a village court (*Gericht*) under an (elected or appointed) mayor

Dorfgericht—a village court

Dreizelgenwirtschaft—a three-field system

Eidgenossenschaft—the Swiss Confederacy

Feuerschauer—fire watch, a village official

Flurzwang—the obligation to collective rather than individual cultivation of fields

Forstbann—(a ruler's) authority over the forest

Forstwart—forest warden, a village official

Fronen—see *Dienste*

Fronhofsgenossenschaft—the association of manorial dependents

Glossary

Gebots- und Verbotsgewalt—a legislative authority; the authority to command and forbid

Gemeinde—a commune, the basic form of self-organization and -government of burghers and peasants (and miners); see *Dorfgemeinde*; *Stadtgemeinde*

Gemeindeversammlung—the assembly of householders in a village commune

Genossenschaft—an association, a structured (and sometimes sworn) association of equal members; see *Eidgenossenschaft*

Gesindezwangsdienst—forced labor (in eastern Germany)

Großgutsherrschaft—in Austria, the large consolidated estate of the early modern era

Gruben- und Pfostenhäuser—rude dwellings composed of an excavation with posts to support the roof

Grundbücher—see *Urbare*

Grundherrschaft—a type of seigneury common in early modern western and southern Germany, where the lands, including demesne, were leased to free or semi-free tenants

gute Polizei—law and order; regulations

Gutsherrschaft—the large consolidated estate of early modern Transelbia, commonly worked by bound labor

Haufen—a troop, a military unit of mercenary infantry or peasant rebels

Haufendorf—a nucleated village

Herrschaft—lordship, in the sense of the authority to rule

Hirten—herdsmen, employed by a village commune

Kreis—a district (literally a circle) or administrative subdivision of a larger unit, as Imperial Circle *(Reichskreis)*

Landgemeinde—a rural commune

Landgericht—a rural district, also the communal organization of the district; a unit of representation in parliamentary states having a peasant estate

Landrecht—territorial law

Landschaft—the parliament of a territory, both its organization into legally defined estates (nobles, prelates, towns, rural districts) and the assembled form of the parliament

Landstände—territorial estates, both individually and assembled in the territorial parliament, or diet

Landtag—a territorial parliament in session; the actual meeting of the *Landschaft*

Lehnschulze—a village mayor who held office for life (Mark Brandenburg); see *Setzschulze*

Obrigkeit—authority, governance, government, both in the sense of the powers of government and in the that of the ruler who holds them

Rat—a council; any elected or coopted body exercising authority

Rechnungsabhör—a financial audit

Reichsstände—the Imperial estates, both individually and assembled in the Imperial Diet

Richter—see *Schöffen*

Salland—a demesne, the part of a manor or estate directly cultivated for the lord

Schöffen—judges of village (and other) courts, also called *Richter* and *Urteiler*

Schöffengericht—a court, urban or rural, staffed by judges called Schöffen

Schollenpflichtigkeit—an obligation to plow, a form of forced labor (in eastern Germany)

Schultheiß—the mayor of a village; also called *Schulze, Ammann,* or *Vogt*

Schulze—see *Schultheiß*

Setzschulze—a village mayor removable at will (Mark Brandenburg); see *Lehnschulze*

Siedlung—a settlement; in a village, the concentration of farmsteads and church

Stadtgemeinde—an urban commune, with or without incorporated guilds

Ständegesellschaft—society based on orders

Ständerhäuser—houses built on stone foundations

Ständestaat—a state based on legally fixed social orders, usually having a parliament

Untergänger—boundary guard, a village official

Urbare—land registers

Urteiler—see *Schöffen*

Glossary

Vergetreidung—the shift from pasture to grain cultivation

Verzelgung—a field rotation system

Villikation—a manor

Vogt—see *Schultheiß*

Wächter—night watch, a village official

Wässerer—waterman, or irrigator, employed by a village commune

Weistum—village customary law, also the written compilation of that law

Zinsbücher—tax registers

Suggestions for Further Reading

A WORK OF THIS KIND does not require a scholarly bibliography, especially since the literature on which it rests was mostly published in German. Instead, this brief essay suggests a few works in English that may be of interest to the reader of *Obedient Germans? A Rebuttal* and helpful to those who want to read more about specific points or the larger setting of this topic.

The classic view of Germany as a case of failed political development appeared in North America during World War I, and it was sharpened and given canonical form by a merger of native arguments and images with the explanations offered by German-speaking writers who had fled Nazi Germany. A characteristic example of this argument is presented by Gordon A. Craig, *The Germans* (New York, 1982; paper reprint), chapter 1. This tradition is subjected to a searching examination by James J. Sheehan, "What Is German History? Reflections on the Role of the *Nation* in German History and Historiography," *Journal of Modern History* 53 (1981): 1–23; Sheehan attacks both its air of tragedy and its teleological-mindedness.

There is, alas, no general history of premodern Germany in English that is up to current standards. For the fourteenth and fifteenth centuries there is F. R. du Boulay, *Germany in the Later Middle Ages* (London, 1981; paper reprint). The succeeding period is more poorly served, for there is nothing more recent than Hajo Holborn, *The Reformation*, vol. 1 of *A History of Modern Germany* (New York 1959; paper reprint), which rests chiefly on pre–1914 scholarship. On the institutions of the Holy Roman Empire, however, one may consult James Allen Vann and Steven W. Rowan, eds., *The Old Reich: Essays on German Political Institutions, 1495–1806* (Brussels, 1974). Although we do not yet have a narrative of premodern German history that takes into account the revisions and advances represented by Blickle's present work, the main directions of research are suggested by two studies, Volker Press, "The Holy Roman Empire in German History," in *Politics and Society in Reformation Europe: Essays for Sir Geoffrey Elton on his Sixty-Fifth Birthday*, edited by E. I. Kouri and Tom Scott (London, 1987), 51–77; and Thomas A. Brady Jr., "Some Peculiarities of German Histories in the Early Modern Era," in *Germania Illustrata: Essays on Early Modern Germany Presented to Gerald Strauss*, edited by Susan C. Karant-Nunn and Andrew Fix (Kirksville MO 1992), 197–216. Both articles describe the rehabilitation of the Holy Roman Empire's image and of German particularism. Some of the revision's implications for comparing German with western European history are spelled out by Thomas A. Brady Jr., "The Rise of Merchant Empires, 1400–1700: A European Counterpoint," in *The Political Economy of Merchant Empires, 1450–1750*, edited by James D. Tracy (Cambridge, 1991; paper reprint), 117–60.

We are better served for the economic and social history of late medieval and early modern Germany, which is the subject of a valuable recent publication: *Germany: A New Social and Economy History*, vol. 1, *1450–1630*, edited by Bob Scribner (London, 1996), and vol. 2, *1630–1800*, edited by Sheilagh Ogilvie (London, 1997). An international team of experts surveys the economic landscapes, population, agrarian economy, diet and consumption, urban networks, markets and marketing, early capitalism, gender and work, social structures, economic and social institutions, communities, daily life, and confessionalism. The contributors document exhaustively the rhythm of crisis, stagnation, recovery, depression, and sustained growth that lies behind Blickle's story.

Because *Obedient Germans? A Rebuttal* draws some concepts from sectors of German historical scholarship poorly known abroad, the most important earlier authors for Blickle's view are not well represented in English. Legal historian Otto von Gierke (1841–1921) has been excerpted in three English publications, of which the central one for this essay is Otto von Gierke, *Community in Historical Perspective: A Translation of Selections from Das deutsche Genossenschaftsrecht (The German Law of Assocations)*, edited by Antony Black (Cambridge, 1990). See also Antony Black, *Guilds and Civil Society in European*

Suggestions for Further Reading

Political Thought from the Twelfth Century to the Present (Ithaca, 1984); and Bob Scribner, "Communities and the Nature of Power," in *Germany*, ed. Scribner, 1:291–325. Of Karl Siegfried Bader's pioneering publications on medieval rural institutions nothing has been translated, and in English there is only his "Approaches to Imperial Reform at the End of the Fifteenth Century," in *Pre-Reformation Germany*, edited and translated by Gerald Strauss (New York, 1972; paper reprint), 73–161.

We are now much better informed about Otto Brunner (1898–1982), whose association with National Socialism did not prevent him from becoming—after his postwar rehabilitation—the most influential medieval historian in the German-speaking world. All the beginner needs to know about Brunner, and much more, is contained in the translators' superb introduction to his major work, *"Land" and Lordship: Structures of Governance in Medieval Austria*, translated by Howard Kaminsky and James Van Horn Melton (Philadelphia, 1992), originally published in German in 1939. For the subject of gender relations, which, though not broached by Brunner, forms a logical extension of his theory of premodern politics, see Merry E. Wiesner, "Gender and the Worlds of Work," in *Germany*, ed. Scribner, 1:209–32. The entire subject of the household and lordship has been transformed by the writings of David W. Sabean, which are cited below.

Under Brunner's influence there emerged since the 1950s a view of premodern German and European history as having been characterized by a social constitution known as the "premodern society based on estates." Those who want to know how European history would read if refashioned according to the Brunnerian concept may consult Dietrich Gerhard, *Old Europe: A Study of Continuity, 1000–1800* (New York: 1981). The concept of "estate" (*Stand*) is developed on a European basis, though with almost exclusive reference to the nobility, by Howard Kaminsky, "Estate, Nobility, and the Exhibition of Estate in the later Middle Ages," *Speculum* 68 (1993): 684–709. On the idea of the "society of estates" or "society of orders," see Roland Mousnier, *Social Hierarchies, 1450 to the Present*, translated by Peter Evans (New York, 1973), which would be most valuable read with Armand Arriaza, "Mousnier and Barber: The Theoretical Underpinnings of the 'Society of Orders,'" *Past and Present*, no. 89 (Nov. 1980): 38–57. The most directly contrary, class-based approach is developed by Robert Brenner, "Agrarian Class Structure and Economic Development in Pre-Industrial Europe," *Past and Present*, no. 70 (Feb. 1976): 30–75.

German institutions of association are presented in a European setting in a volume edited by Peter Blickle, *Communalism, Representation, Resistance* (Oxford, 1997), which contains comparative studies on rural and urban communes and on parliamentary institutions. Many of the territorial parliaments in the Holy Roman Empire are studied by F. L. Carsten, *Princes and Parliaments in Germany from the Fifteenth to the Eighteenth Century* (Oxford, 1959), but there is no study of the imperial parliament in English. For communal institutions, both rural and urban, the best introduction in English is Peter Blickle, *The Communal Reformation: The People's Quest for Salvation in Sixteenth-Century Germany*, translated by Thomas Dunlap (Atlantic Highlands NJ, 1992).

There is a growing literature in English on premodern German rural history that perforce treats the relations between peasants and territorial rulers highlighted by *Obedient Germans? A Rebuttal*. Basic studies include Hermann Rebel, *Peasant Classes: The Bureaucratization of Property and Family Relations under Early Habsburg Absolutism, 1511–1636* (Princeton, 1983); Thomas N. Robisheaux, *Rural Society and the Search for Order in Early Modern Germany* (Cambridge, 1989); David W. Sabean, *Power in the Blood: Popular Culture and Village Discourse in Early Modern Germany* (Cambridge, 1984; paper reprint); and Tom Scott, *Freiburg and the Breisgau: Town-Country Relations in the Age of Reformation and Peasants' War* (Oxford, 1986). In a class by itself, though contributing powerfully to the general tendency to disrupt the state-centered narrative, is David W. Sabean's pioneering village study in two volumes, *Property, Production, and Family in Neckarhausen* (Cambridge, 1991; paper reprint); and *Kinship in Neckarhausen* (Cambridge, 1997).

German urban history has a relatively rich literature in English. On the urban communes in the Middle Ages, see Heinz Stoob, "The Role of the Civic Community in Central European Urban Development during the Twelfth to the Fifteenth Centuries," translated by S. Gold, *Transactions of the Ancient Monuments Society* 23 (1978/79): 67–91; Fritz Rorig, *The Medieval Town*, translated by D. Bryant (Berkeley, 1967; paper reprint); and Hans-Christoph Rublack, "Political and Social Norms in Urban Communities in the Holy Roman Empire," in *Religion, Politics, and Social Protest*, edited by Kaspar von

Greyerz (London, 1984), 24–60. For the following centuries there is one important study of the revitalization of communalism in the Reformation era by Bernard Moeller, *Imperial Cities and the Reformation: Three Essays*, translated by H. C. Erik Midelfort and Mark U. Edwards Jr. (Philadelphia, 1975; paper reprint). A number of the works on individual towns emphasize the social and institutional aspects studied by Blickle, among them Thomas A. Brady, *Ruling Class, Regime and Reformation at Strasbourg, 1520–1555* (Leiden, 1978); Susan C. Karant-Nunn, *Zwickau in Transition, 1500–1547: The Reformation as an Agent of Change* (Columbus, 1987); Christopher R. Friedrichs, *Urban Society in an Age of War: Nördlingen, 1580–1720* (Princeton, 1979); Gerald L. Soliday, *A Community in Conflict: Frankfurt Society in the Seventeenth and Early Eighteenth Centuries* (Hanover NH, 1974); and Lee Palmer Wandel, *Always among Us: Images of the Poor in Zwingli's Zurich* (Cambridge, 1990).

The subject of revolts, which plays such a large part in Blickle's little book, enjoys a relatively rich literature in English. For help with the literature, see R. W. Scribner, "Peasant Politics in Early Modern Europe: A Review Article," *Comparative Studies in Society and History* 28 (1986): 248–54; and Tom Scott, "Community and Conflict in Early Modern Germany: Review Article," *European History Quarterly* 16 (1986): 209–17. The medieval rural revolts are well covered by Peter Blickle, "Peasant Revolts in the German Empire in the Late Middle Ages" *Social History* 4 (1979): 223–40. The rural revolts of the early modern era in general are treated in Peter Blickle, "The Criminalization of Peasant Resistance in the Holy Roman Empire: Toward a History of the Emergence of High Treason in Germany," *Journal of Modern History* 58 (1986): supplement, S88–S97; Thomas N. Robisheaux, "Peasant Unrest and the Moral Economy in the German Southwest 1560–1620," *Archive for Reformation History* 78 (1987): 174–86; and Winfried Schulze, "Peasant Resistance in Sixteenth- and Seventeenth-Century Germany in a European Context," in *Religion, Politics, and Social Protest*, edited by Kaspar von Greyerz (London, 1984), 61–98.

The great German Peasants' War of 1525 is especially richly documented in English. The leading interpretation is Peter Blickle, *The Revolution of 1525: The German Peasants' War from a New Perspective*, translated by Thomas A. Brady Jr. and H. C. Erik Midelfort (Baltimore, 1981; paper reprint); a selection of secondary literature is translated and edited by Bob Scribner and Gerhard Benecke, *The German Peasant War: New Views* (London, 1979; paper reprint); and a splendid anthology of the most important documents is translated and edited by Tom Scott and Bob Scribner, *The German Peasants' War: A History in Documents* (Atlantic Highlands NJ, 1991; paper reprint).

Urban revolts are treated by F. L. Carsten, "Medieval Democracy in the Brandenburg Towns and Its Defeat in the Fifteenth Century," *Transactions of the Royal Historical Society 25* (1943): 73–91 (an older study still worth consulting); Rhiman Rotz, "Urban Uprisings in Germany: Revolutionary or Reformists? The Case of Brunswick, 1374," *Viator 4* (1973): 207–23; and Christopher R. Friedrichs, "German Town Revolts and the Seventeenth-Century Crisis," *Renaissance and Modern Studies 26* (1982): 27–51.

Blickle's area of concern in *Obedient Germans? A Rebuttal* is from 1300 to the end of the Holy Roman Empire just after 1800. The setting of the tale's end and the transition to the nineteenth-century situation receives magisterial treatment in the hands of James J. Sheehan, *German History, 1770–1866* (Oxford, 1989; paper reprint). The concept and institutions of the empire are studied by John Gagliardo, *The Holy Roman Empire as Idea nd Reality, 1763–1806* (Bloomington IN, 1980). The major issues involved in the dissolution of the old rural society are addressed in a general context by Jerome Blum, *The End of the Old Order in Rural Europe* (Princeton, 1978); in a Prussian context by Robert M. Berdahl, *The Politics of the Prussian Nobility: The Development of a Conservative Ideology, 1770–1848* (Princeton, 1988; paper reprint); and in an Austrian context by E. M. Link, *The Emancipation of the Austrian Peasantry, 1740–1798* (New York, 1949). Most studies of smaller states often give some attention to rural life, including James Allen Vann, *The Making of a State: Württemberg, 1593–1793* (Ithaca, 1984); Charles W. Ingrao, *The Hessian Mercenary State: Ideas, Institutions, and Reform under Frederick II, 1760–1785* (Cambridge, 1987). Aristocratic and bourgeois ideas about the peasantry and its political potential are analyzed by John Gagliardo, *From Pariah to Patriot: The Changing Image of the German Peasant, 1770–1840* (Lexington KY, 1969), but for a perspective from the ground up on modernization, one must begin with the studies by David W. Sabean, noted above.

That the burghers' traditional politics were irrelevant, perhaps even harmful, to a modern political culture, is one of the central dogmas of German historiography. It has been seriously challenged only by Mack Walker, *German Home Towns: Community, State, and General Estate, 1648–1871* (Ithaca, 1971), one of the most imaginative studies on Germany history written in English. Walker's approach fits well with the argument of *Obedient Germans? A Rebuttal.* Another study that bears on this question is T. C. W. Blanning, *Reform and Revolution in Mainz, 1743–1803* (Cambridge, 1974).

It is generally agreed that modern German ideas about politics and history began to form during the last third of the eighteenth century in the Age of Enlightenment, but there is no agreement about how that happened. The larger political culture rooted in local rights and experiences is treated by Mack Walker, *Johann Jakob Moser and the Holy Roman Empire of the German Nation* (Chapel Hill, 1981); and Jonathan B. Knudsen, *Justus Möser and the German Enlightenment* (Cambridge, 1986). Peter Blickle, in *Obedient Germans? A Rebuttal*, argues that the deep tradition of local self-government and defense of local rights in Germany gave rise to a popular idea of liberty, of which the best philosophical formulation was produced by Jean-Jacques Rousseau. The finest empirical expositions of the conceptual potential of local experience are by Renate Blickle, "Appetitus Libertatis: A Social Historial Approach to the Development of the Earliest Human Rights: The Example of Bavaria," in *Human Rights and Cultural Diversity: Europe—Arabic-Islamic World—Africa—China*, edited by Wolfgang Schmale (Goldbach, 1993), 143–62; and "From Subsistence to Property: Traces of a Fundamental Change in Early Modern Bavaria," translated by Thomas N. Robisheaux, *Central European History* 25 (1992): 377–86. Each works more or less against the traditionally dominant view, which holds that in Germany the idea of freedom arose in a purely philosophical context, not a political one as elsewhere in western Europe. German political ideas and notions, it has been believed, were divorced from political action and experience, and the disjunction between the idea of freedom and political action doomed the German middle class or German liberalism to tragic failure. A classic statement of this view is Leonard Krieger, *The German Idea of Freedom: History of a Political Idea* (Boston, 1957; paper reprint); and one can get essentially the same story from Klaus Epstein, *The Genesis of German Conservatism* (Princeton, 1966; paper reprint).

Index

Index

Index

Index